Front cover:
Original sketch of Swiz cursive logo
Circa 1989
Art: Jason Farrell

Previous spread:
CBGB, New York, NY
September 17, 1989
Photos: John Hiltz

Published by Akashic Books

ISBN: 978-1-63614-265-4
Library of Congress Control Number: 2025933701
Second printing

EU Authorized Representative details:
Easy Access System Europe
Mustamäe tee 50, 10621 Tallinn, Estonia
gpsr.request@easproject.com

Akashic Books, Brooklyn, New York
Instagram, X, Facebook: AkashicBooks
info@akashicbooks.com
www.akashicbooks.com

EQQUS: ACT I

. . . it's a *swiz*, it seems to be offering you something, but actually it's taking something away. Your intelligence and your concentration, every minute . . .

I don't want to sound like a spoilsport, old chum—but there really is no substitute for reading.

—*Excerpt from* Equus *by Peter Shaffer*, © *1973*.

SWIZ BOOK

WORDS BY:

Alex Daniels

Jason Farrell

Nathan Larson

Amanda MacKaye

Dave Stern

Shawn Brown

Ramsey Metcalf

SELECT INTERVIEWS CONDUCTED BY:

Anthony Pappalardo ✷

John Scharbach †

SELECT PORTIONS PREVIOUSLY PUBLISHED IN:

Radio Silence / A Selected Visual History of American Hardcore Music ❖

Bells of.. *00/85* liner notes ❄

Punk Planet #30 ✣

Shining Life #9 ✦

BOOK DESIGN BY:

Jason Farrell

DEDICATED TO THE DEPARTED MENTIONED HEREIN:

Chip Cashel

Michael & Elaine Daniels

Lou Gigger

Kevin Fuckin' Haley

John Stabb

Steve Stern

Ginger & Bill MacKaye

Barbara Jean Metcalf

Marcus Wilcoxon

THANK YOU

FOREWORD

Swiz was a Washington, D.C., hardcore punk band that existed from April of 1987 through August of 1990, during which time they played roughly 100 shows, wrote 35 songs, and released one 7" and two 12" vinyl records. Two more 7" records and a compilation CD were released in the three years immediately following their dissolution.

This collection of writing is not meant to expand on those statistics.

Alex, Sanctuary Theater, Washington, D.C.
January 9, 1988
Photo: Andy Meissner

ROCK
TO
SWIZ.

Chapter 1

OVERTURE

ALL THIS IS

recalled as truth but
can't quite be called
fact

It's been left
as it was pulled
raw from memory
with its tendency
to distort

It is at best 100%
emotionally factual
for this moment

—*SWIZ*

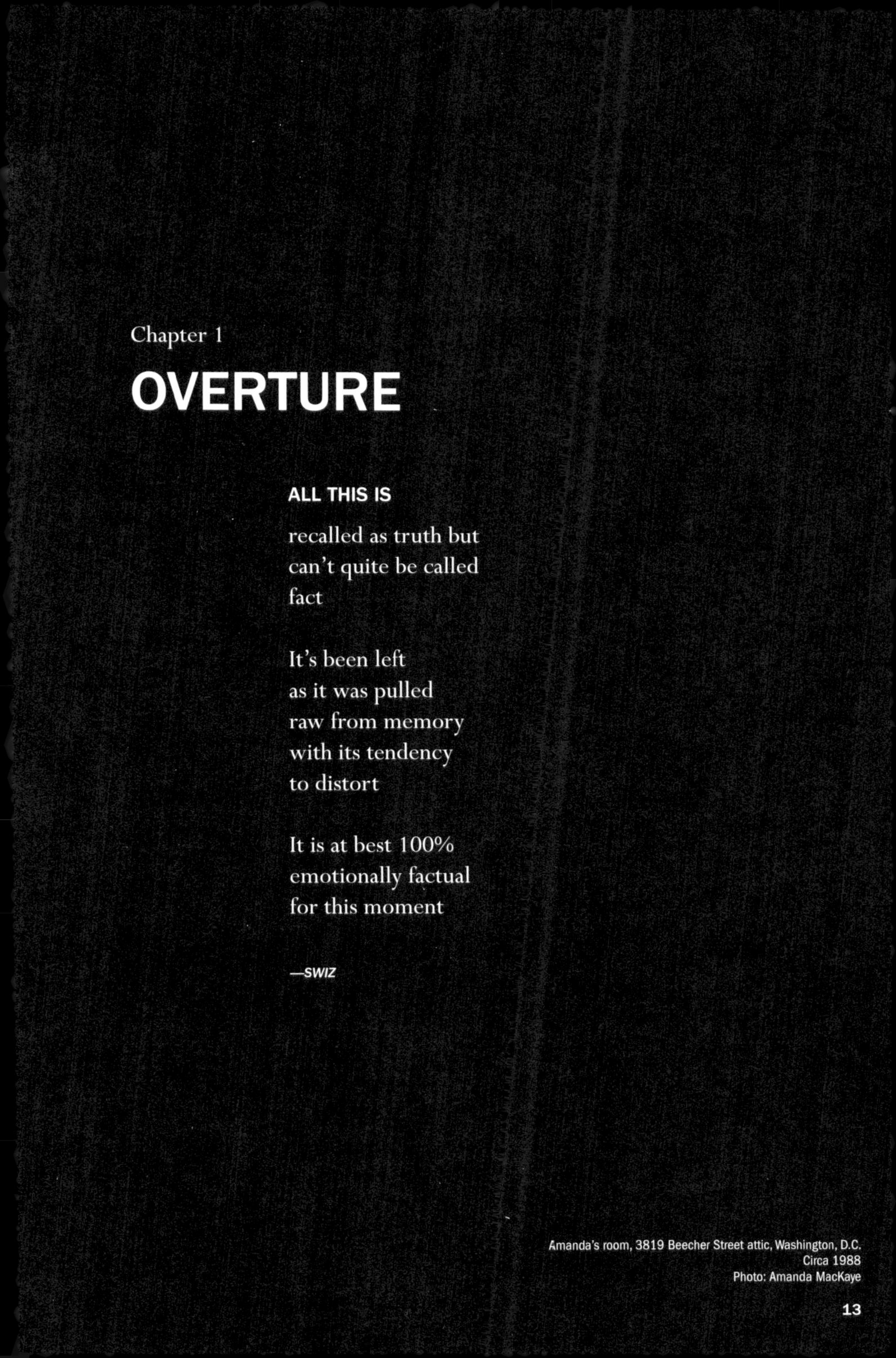

Amanda's room, 3819 Beecher Street attic, Washington, D.C.
Circa 1988
Photo: Amanda MacKaye

COLLECTION: 1

I remember wandering around the brightly lit streets of Montreal, not caring where I was or whether we'd get lost because I was with my guys and everything would be fine.

I remember freaking out when Matt and Bill Dolan almost came to blows under some overpass as the tour crumbled apart.

I remember arriving in San Francisco for the first time and marveling at how dirty and old it seemed, because I had some notion that everything in California must be bright and shiny.

I remember the crowd reeling backwards several feet when we let out our first chord opening for Public Enemy because that night we had it together, and we were loud.

I remember meeting up with the Gorilla Biscuits in a club parking lot in California during the Golden Hour, and thinking that I was part of something that was moving forward fast and had a definite use-by date.

—ALEX

HOT GHOST: NEVADA 1988

The dipstick was dry . . . just a bit of black gristle on its tip. The gas station guy whistled and half listened as we backtracked across a thousand miles of symptoms and excuses, each hiccup and skip. That time in Toronto when the van wouldn't go . . . but then suddenly it did. The smell of hot metal as we rolled off the Rockies, coasting in neutral to save gas.

As he wiped down the stick he conceded it wasn't right—supposed to be up under the hood, long as a sword, not hidden below the engine shroud like a lost pocketknife.

"But still . . . you shoudla looked a little harder."

He filled the hole with red fluid, though his face showed he knew it wouldn't do no good. Stabbed the stick back in and said, "See, the thing about transmissions is . . ." and then said some other things I missed cause I was watching him fit the doghouse back over the engine. I guess I'd never noticed it had been so close, a hot ghost sitting shotgun in the cab.

Shawn and Amanda wandered back with Cokes and cheap snacks. We all piled back in the van, negotiated seats, and the collective mood brightened in the process. The van managed to lurch forward so we resumed the long trip out of the desert, luck and denial our secret weapons. I turned to see if the gas guy was waving us off, but only saw his back.

—JASON

ALL MY LIES ARE TRUE: PART 1

Scene: The driveway in front of the Daniels's house, summer 1988. Teenagers are milling around a van with nervous excitement. It's early in the morning for this nighttime crew. A sunny, clear morning filled with possibility.

I arrive. *(How did I get there? I live miles from Alex's house. Do I have a bag of some sort? Surely I packed??)* We all exchange requisite greetings as Alex's parents appear. Mrs. Daniels sees me in obvious expression of someone about to get in the van with not just her son, but rather a rowdy group of boys. She takes a step toward me. With eyes wide and a look of shock coming over her spirit, she says: "YOU are going *with* them??"

Scene: Flash forward a few decades. The MacKaye family is gathered around the dinner table for one of their Sunday gatherings. Dad is at the command chair listening to the chatter of his kids. They are talking about travel and the three youngest are comparing/exchanging reflections on touring in the United States. It's a noisy, crowded and warm room with lots of movement. Amanda has just finished some tale of a time with Swiz.

A look of confusion, no, concern maybe, comes over Dad's face and he shifts in his seat. He begins to speak over the chatter and the talkers turn their volume down. Without a direct address to me he says, "Your mother and I let you go on tour when you were in high school?" with a punctuation of disbelief.

(End)

—*AMANDA*

LOVE

I remember feeling detached from the music of Swiz. It was hard to believe people I knew so well were creating something I loved so much. I loved the way the songs sounded. I loved it like a listener. I loved the way my bass sounded. Sometimes. Mostly it was a shitty bass sound, but the notes. I loved the notes. I loved how they fit in with Alex Shawn Jason. I loved playing Nathan songs. I love punk. I love its aesthetic. I love our aloofness while the others think punks are trash & fools. I love how somehow punk is still a secret. It was a different secret then. But it still feels full of value and beautiful as I teach it to my kids.

When we played shows we used to bring my guitar cabinet as an extra to set up on my side of the stage. I hated the monitors, all I really needed was hearing Jason's Les Paul.

Imagine going anywhere on the planet. As long as you find the punks, everyone you meet is cool. Because they all know the language and sound of punk. I love that this is possible. Even if they all don't know the name of your band, they all know the sound of a JCM 800, even though they don't know its name. I love the sound of a JCM 800.

I loved the process of writing the songs. Figuring out my parts. I changed Nathan's line in "Dimluck." I think Jason was bummed, but he tolerated it. Maybe I did it to make some of the stuff more mine. It was only to be heard live that way. Sounded more punk to me anyhow.

I kinda hated/was scared of recording the *With Dave* 7". Felt like a foreign environment. No audience. No sweat. No dark. All focus on my turn. Jason could effortlessly swim laps in a studio. It was second nature.

I loved watching Fury record at Inner Ear with Don. Something was happening. Something was being etched, something that might last. I wondered if that was the first gig Chris Thomson had singing. I wished I'd been playing the bass but I loved seeing Shawn do it.

—DAVE

GOOD AFTERNOON;

I have been contacted regarding a prospective *Swiz* feature film. Before discussion can move further, we would need to secure indicated locations and items in order to guarantee authenticity/period accuracy.

It goes without saying all former band members would need to be consulted re: needed locations/ objects, etc.

Please advise + confirm availability of below.
Contact if any questions arise.

Thanks and best wishes,
NL

LOCATIONS, INT.:

Alex's car
Multiple basements, primarily Jason's folks, Bethesda, MD
Community Center, Hattiesburg Miss., USA
Multiple bedrooms, Washington, D.C. / Mont. County, MD

LOCATIONS, EXT.:

Rest stop "Dolly Madison" I-95 NJ Turnpike
Parking lot, Berkeley, CA
Parking lot, Fort Worth, TX
Parking lot, F and 9th streets NW Washington, D.C.
Parking lot, Blockbuster Video, Chevy Chase, MD
Parking lot, Columbus, OH
Parking lot, Radio Shack, Boise, ID
Parking lot, Shoney's, Knoxville, TN

PROPS

Boom box by Realistic w duct tape

(3) Normal bias Maxwell cassette tapes

- Side A Bad Brains / Side B Metallica
- Side A Circle Jerks / Side B Fear
- Side A Big Black / Side B Black Flag

(1) Soul Braid™ hair extension, tangled in
Fender Precision bass headstock tuning pegs

(1) T-shirt screen and squeegee

(1) Marshall head perched precariously,
speaker cable frayed and pulled tight

(1) Xerox machine / copies 5¢ per

(1) Shure 58 microphone (battered) / tangled + knotted XLR cable

(3-6) Blown tires

(1) Tattoo gun

(1) Change machine

(1) Colt 45 32oz malt liquor bottle

(4) Crushed Jolt Cola cans / van floor

(1) Case, 24 bottles coconut Yoo-Hoo

(2) Dunlop guitar pick(s): 1.0mm black / .73mm gray, chewed

(1) Super Hold Aqua Net aerosol can, 10 oz

(1) Tub Queen Helene / LA Looks / Dippity-Do hair gel

(2) Glass fuse, 4Amp Slo Blow

(1) Tube Super Glue

(1) Pack Hanes white Ts

(1) Pair Vans, blue/black

(5-10) Plywood stage(s)

(1) Pair burgundy Toughskins

(1) Pair drumsticks, halved

(1) Broken headstock, Gibson SG '70s vintage

(1) Blue pleather bench for van, removed

—NATHAN

PURE

It was crazy because I was just a kid hanging out, then I became the singer of Dag Nasty, then all of a sudden I wasn't the singer of Dag Nasty. For a minute I wondered what I was going to do next. I was almost expected to do something next, so I really had to think what I wanted to do.

Then Ramsey approached me about doing a band with Jason Farrell and I was really comfortable with that because I knew Jason as the kid from the skateboard store—we'd say what's up to each other—we weren't tight yet, but I was really comfortable with him . . . and then with all of them because they were all cool.

All of us in Swiz shared a very tight bond, we were all roughly the same age and wanted the same things. We didn't have any real aspirations, we weren't really trying to do anything with it, it was just playing music . . . It was pure, we weren't thinking it would become some serious thing, I was just experiencing it.

—SHAWN ✷✦

Shawn, CBGB, New York, NY
September 17, 1989
Photo: John Hiltz

Chapter 2

LARVAL

BLACK

I grew up in a white middle-class county in the suburbs of Maryland. There were maybe three other black kids in my school, other times I was the only one. So you learn to cope at a young age. At that point in life I had already made a decision that I was going to be cool with whoever is cool with me. It was that simple. I made that choice really early on. The hardcore scene was just a little reflection of how the whole world was at the time. I don't feel that it was any different.

—SHAWN ✷✦

Shawn
Circa 1974
Photo: P.G. County Public School System

LATE BLOOMER

I lived in Upper Marlboro until 2nd grade and then moved to Bethesda. My folks were music fans and stressed the importance of learning to play an instrument when I was little. Some of it didn't stick. While my brother was a serious composition and cello student, my outings with the violin and clarinet fizzled. But I loved music. When I was about 5 or 6, my cousin sat me down with Bachman Turner Overdrive's *Not Fragile* album and the first Chicago Transit Authority double LP (a classic) and pointed out each musician pictured, explaining what each member brought to the group. I kept a sketchbook and drew pictures of rock groups, expecting to be in one someday.

My brother, having gotten into jazz and fusion, took me to the Kool Jazz Festival at the Kennedy Center in D.C. in 7th grade, where I saw Sun Ra, Archie Shepp, Art Blakey, and others. So at this time, I was heavily into classic rock and jazz. My sister introduced punk in 7th grade, mostly through the 2 Tone ska movement—she brought home *Dance Craze* and I started to get into the Specials, English Beat, Selecter and then other associated acts, like Elvis Costello . . . and then eventually other groups that were either "alternative" (R.E.M.) or going big (the Police). Pretty soon punk started seeping into my record collection, and then *Singles Going Steady* hooked me completely.

Being in the suburbs of D.C. allowed me to see some of these big acts when they played. But it wasn't until about 10th grade that I became aware that there was a local music scene. My friend Andy Kaufman and I played in a band called Little Albert. Once, during a printmaking class, he played me a tape of Gray Matter's "I Am the Walrus" cover (years later I played in a band with Gray Matter's guitarist, Mark Haggerty). Hearing their punk cover of a Beatles song was amazing. Where did they record this? Where do they play? Do people see them play?

The answers to all of those questions would be made clear over the next few years. My brother, again a musical guide, took me to see 9353 at d.c. space, a bar/restaurant where bands played on a tiny stage. It was 1985. I was in 10th grade, and it felt really adult to be out in the city at a club. I was totally intimidated by the city, the grown-ups at the show, the "punkness" of it all . . . Before the bands, we talked to a fellow named Lou Gigger, the guitarist for the opening act, Braille Party. His band had an album called *Welcome to Maryland*. He was the nicest fellow . . . just friendly chitchat before he played. His band was fun. 9353 was an otherworldly performance. Probably about the best show I've ever seen.

I was a kid deeply into music. I lived in a rich suburb that was near a city that had large swaths of land that had not been redeveloped since the 1968 riots. I was tired of my private school and wanted to experience something beyond my varsity sports, dances and college applications. I got some of that from the utterly transfixing, transformative music made by people like 9353 . . . but I also got kind of a friendly invitation from people like Lou. Sure, this is a gritty, urban, exciting and creative space . . . but it also has aspects and personalities that are familiar. In other words, great music can be played by people who are like you. There is a big world out there that you can contribute to and soak in. I learned that if you dig deeper into it, you will find more . . . more exciting music and culture, as well as aspects of the bigger world that aren't tailor-made for a sheltered high school student.

Meeting Derek Denckla opened me up to the D.C. punk scene. Derek's brother was friends with my brother. Derek needed a drummer for his band and so I joined him, Chad Houseknecht, and Ravi Ricker in Carpe Diem. Derek was a very soulful, creative kid, who seemed really grown up at the time, in that he had a creative vision, and actually took actions to see his plans through.

With Carpe Diem, I played shows at Dupont Circle at an armed forces protest put on by a local activist group called Positive Force; the Complex, which was a big club that had huge punk shows for about a year or so; and at local suburban community centers.

At one Positive Force benefit at the Bethesda Community Center, Carpe Diem played with NFC, Stüge (future members of Shudder to Think), Bells of.. (which later put out *11:11*, one of my favorite albums ever), Gray Matter, and Dag Nasty (during their Dave Smalley era). Though Jason was in Bells of.., I didn't meet him that day. But I met loads of other young punks including Andy Rapoport and Kevin Haley—two of the nicest people one could ever meet in what seemed like a totally adult, challenging environment (I was a late bloomer!). This multiband bill really showcased the extent of creativity going on in my hometown, and illuminated for me the accessibility and friendliness of the people putting it all together.

This was right after "Revolution Summer," in which people in bands in D.C. really tried to redefine the scene as a creative, revolutionary moment, rather than a violent, retrograde, cookie-cutter scene. In the wake of this flourishing of expression, a lot of suburban private school kids like me got wind of what was going on, met other kids who wanted to create, and set about doing it.

Derek had a friend who was putting together a tape comp called *The Balloon Races*, and we recorded some songs for it. NFC was also on the comp, and that's how I met Nathan. His band was breaking up, and Carpe Diem was finished because Derek and Ravi left D.C. for college. Nathan and I got along, and we decided to become a bass-and-drums duo in search of a band. We jammed with a few guitarists—Scott Crawford, Andy Cone, Ron Wolfe—but kept on looking for a good fit.

—ALEX†

DAG NASTY

GRAYMATTER

BELLS OF

- N.F.C. -

STÜGE CARPI DIEM

FOUNDATION (13)

7 BANDS — 5 BUCKS!!

BETHESDA COMMUNITY CENTER 5-10 p.m.

SAT. 29th

Show flyer
March 29, 1986
Courtesy of Ben Pekkanen

In the summer after 4th grade my friend Marcus took me to the Audubon Sanctuary, a big arboretum and nature preserve near his house. He knew of an entrance around the back of the property, like a window or raised Dutch door in the chain-link fence that we could lift our bikes through.

Mine was a stripped-down novelty Evel Knievel bike. It had been stolen from my backyard the summer before and ditched in some bushes around the corner. I had found it again over the winter when the leaves were gone; I could see the frame pipes like dirty white bones in the woven sticks. I think Morris Minter took it, but have no proof . . . just a feeling. He was an older kid who in my mind had a mustache and a brown suede jacket with a matching hippie hat, walked around with a cane for a while. He was probably 12 at that time, but I always rounded up older kids to full-grown adults even when they were just a few grades up.

I was psyched to have my bike back, but the novelty gas tank and shocks wouldn't go unnoticed by the older kids with legit Schwinn Scramblers—they'd heckle a kid just for having a Huffy. So after pulling the vines and fixing the flats, Marcus and I ripped all the fake shit off and spray-painted the frame yellow. If I rode by fast it could maybe pass as a Sting-Ray.

But it was fucking heavy . . . I had to strain to get it up in that Dutch door. I scraped it through, leaving a chalky trail of bright yellow paint on the dull fence pole. Once inside we rode around the winding back paths, shaded from the sun by lush trees, steering clear of the buildings in the front to avoid getting kicked out. It felt like being somewhere else completely . . . away from the rows of squat brick houses where neighborhood kids jockeyed for dominance.

They had all kinds of trees in there, including Japanese maples whose leaves looked a lot like pot. We thought maybe that could get you high, too—as if the leaf shape had something to do with it—so we snapped a big branch and left it hanging to die and dry out.

> *During that previous summer, around the time my bike was stolen, the teen girl who babysat me and my sisters thought it would be funny to get us high. I was eight. We didn't know any better—we liked her a lot—plus she seemed so excited*

about it that we said OK. She skipped off to her hiding spot and came back with a tiny roach in her palm. It didn't do much, as it was just a roach between us three, and our parents never found out . . . but what a fucked-up thing to do to a kid.

In hindsight it was kind of a fucked-up time in Bethesda. We had a lot of independence very early on—little kids in a rush to catch up to the older neighborhood kids who seemed cool by default. We'd circle them on our bikes with an ear bent to their bragging, hanging around like flies they'd swat from time to time. Standard stuff, but those older kids we wanted to emulate were deep in the leftover mental residue of late-'60s drug culture.

We went back to the Audubon a week later, stuffed all the dried leaves in a big Ziploc bag, then took it back to Marcus's underground fort to test the stash. Being fresh out of 4th grade we hadn't been properly high yet, so we couldn't really say if it was working . . . but it *did* smell a lot like pot when it burned.

Marcus thought we could sell it, and figured his older friend Roger Marbury might want it. Now that Roger was in jr. high he didn't hang out with Marcus anymore, spending most of his time with his new friend Colin Sears . . . but we figured it was worth a shot.

Colin lived in my neighborhood, a couple streets over from my house, so we biked there with our throw-pillow-sized bag of fake pot and knocked on his door. Marcus worked the deal, saying, "It's not pot, but it looks and smells a lot like it, so it might get you a little high. Try it . . . if you like it, then pay us some money." Roger and Colin said OK, but in hindsight Colin probably would have said anything just to shoo us the fuck off his dad's porch as quickly as possible.

We swung back by the next week to collect money or the rest of the stuff but Colin said he threw it all out because it just gave him a headache.

It would be another eight years before Colin and I finally managed to get some business dealings going in earnest; we started Hellfire Records together as a shell company to launder vinyl for Swiz and his Dag Nasty side hustle, Blood Bats.

—JASON

THE P.G. COUNTY MALL TEST

I stumbled upon Matt Ray in what I would call my new wave phase . . . punk-curious, you know what I mean? Matt was the kid that would give me, like, Bad Brains and the Circle Jerks stuff—introduced me to that culture. I'd seen videos with Devo, and the whole skater thing going on there. So I was like, "OK, skateboarders are cool, I had one when I was younger. Wow, I know who Tony Alva is . . . I saw him on *Wild World of Sports* . . . so maybe I should check this out." Because I mean, that's the whole thing with skateboarding . . . it was a physical activity, but it wasn't jock shit. It was a representation of culture, too.

All of those things, from my perspective of where I was coming from, were big social and lifestyle changes. They were like making a statement. Being punk out here was definitely not cool . . . Hyattsville had more of a working-class tradition. "You fucking spent money to fuck up your hair? . . . The fuck is wrong with you?!" You know, that type of thing. Also, it was very Catholic in that area. So they're very robotic and, you know, they're adherents to like fucking societal and religious standards, which is something early on as a kid I just started to buck against because it didn't make fucking sense to me; it's kind of what led me to punk rock in the first place. And really, being punk rock was just being an asshole in their eyes. You couldn't go to P.G. Plaza, they'd definitely kick you out of there. Matter of fact, we would go to places to see how punk we were.

"Are we punk enough to get kicked out of the fucking mall?"

"We are! We're doing it right!"

—SHAWN

HYATTSVILLE

I think me and Eliza and Matt Ray were hanging out . . . we met Eddie Diaz, who was talking about, "Yeah, this kid Ian Svenonius lives over here, blah, blah." I remember trying to jockey around the neighborhood to I see if I can run into this fucking kid, the only other punk kid in my town. I need more knowledge, you know what I mean? I need to be with more of my people.

I didn't even know punk rock was really happening in D.C. until I met Svenonius. He's like, "Oh yeah, that's going on right down the road." While Matt had given me general punk stuff, Svenonius was giving me Faith and Minor Threat.

I met Stuart *(Hill, later from Shudder to Think)* through Ian, and we all went to as many shows as possible together from then on.

—SHAWN

Shawn, Wilson Center, Washington, D.C.
August 3, 1984
Photos: Mary Diaz

AGGRESSIVELY AGREEING

Jason and Marcus Wilcoxon's locker was next to John Garrish and mine in 8th grade. John and I rode our BMX bikes up to Marcus's house on Jones Bridge Road. John had heard a bunch of post-eighth/pre-9th graders had a skateboard ramp. Pedaling up the hill to the ramp, I could hear skate sounds. They were completely unfamiliar. Tweenish-ers yelling (my kids call it "aggressively agreeing"). It sounded like everybody was aggressively agreeing. We got there. All of them completely abusing a 1/2-moon wood structure. Punk throwing itself outta a radio. Big Boys, Circle Jerks, Black Flag?—one of 'em. On top of a hill in a field, a slightly spooky house on the left, scattered trees around (Marcus's house). This was the exact moment I found my correct life direction. I think I bought my Race Inc. from Jason? Now I had to get rid of this thing and replace it with a skateboard.

—DAVE

(Left to right)
Jason, Unknown, Marcus Wilcoxon, Chevy Chase, MD
Fall 1983
Photo: Dave Stern

NO BMX

JR. HIGH, PART 1: PERFECT HAIR

In my 40s I helped Kathleen Hanna
lay out her record cover
asked if she remembered
my sister Shanda

A couple weeks later
I then asked my sister
if she might remember
Kathleen

With the same kind of sigh
they gave the same answer:
"Oh my god,
she had the best wings in junior high"

—JASON

JR. HIGH, PART 2: 7 MINUTES

In 7th grade at a make-out party I got randomly paired with my backyard neighbor Christina Billotte and dispatched to the closet for 7 minutes in heaven. We sat on the floor among the boots and hanging coats; not kissing, just talking . . . nothing about punk rock . . . we didn't know anything yet.

—JASON

(Clockwise from top left)
Kath een Hanna, Shanda Farrell, Jason Farrell, Christina Billotte
Excerpt from 1981-82 Westland "Wildcats" yearbook

CORT

My mom bought me my first bass as I recall at an actual record store in a mall, which was overpriced at something like $75; a blue Cort with a palsied neck, strings about 4 inches off the fretboard. I thought they were all like that, and mused, *Shit, this is even more difficult than I anticipated.* Barely able to press the strings down hard enough to produce any kind of tone, with great effort I learned "LOUIE LOUIE," assuming it was a Black Flag song. I'd plug my Cort into the home stereo, that kind of worked; I could hear it in one speaker, faintly. Then I got myself a . . .

GORILLA

amp . . . It sounded like shit but it was better than the stereo.

NFC

There were three or four other punks at my jr. high, a public school in suburban Maryland that was populated mostly by jocks and future Republican senatorial aides, so we had no choice really but to be in each other's company. I used Knox gelatin to get my hair in an approximation of glue-spikes . . . the gelatin I would painstakingly mix myself in the boys' bathroom prior to school.

We started a band called NFC which either stood for No Friends Club or, when seasonally appropriate, Nothing For Christmas. We played "LOUIE LOUIE" because that was what we knew. Then we learned "WILD THING!" which was the same song with different words. We wrote a song called "I HATE YOU!" which was "LOUIE LOUIE!" (or "WILD THING!") with yet another set of lyrics to puff out our set. We got a show with a bunch of other bands at the local community center and I thought, *Shit, I'd better get a . . .*

PEAVEY

bass amp, called a TNT. The guitarist had a Peavey Bandit so you could say we were fully PEAVEY-POWERED. The rad thing about my amp was that we could also plug in our Tandy vocal mic, which we'd picked up at RadioShack and was a silver plastic thing, the kind that had an on/off switch. Then I got . . .

A REAL BASS

This was a big deal, because it was about $250. I found it in the classifieds, and my folks, who saw where all this was heading, very very hesitantly got the thing for me, after much cajoling. It was and probably still is a thing of beauty: a mid-'60s Olympic-white Fender Precision, which on the current market would fetch about $4,500, if not more. Around 1990 I was to abandon it in a rehearsal space in the East Village; I didn't want to go back and get it cos I was fighting with the guy who owned the place and I was too much of a pussy, forever to my deep regret.

With the bass came a Sunn amp which was a big solid-state monster, inferior to the more expensive Ampeg SVT but still pretty good. I paired it with a cabinet I bought off Wendell from Iron Cross in an exchange that felt very much like a drug deal about to go very wrong.

Pretty quickly one realizes (harkening back to the cover of *London Calling*) that you'd better not smash anything, much less your hard-earned equipment. One of the highest aspirations you can have in a band is to get to the point where your equipment can be easily smashed (and quickly replaced) without sweat, and this status seemed infinitely far off . . . but it's good to have goals.

—*NATHAN*

THAT WEIRD SCRATCHINESS

We'd skip school and make big expeditions out to the record store knowing that we had to make it home before our parents; it would take you an hour and a half just to get there. It was a day of planning just to time the buses. You'd go to Y&T where Ian and Guy worked and there would be so many rad records there; you'd have 20 records out and only 30 bucks so you're trying to sort through them and decide which ones to get.

That weird scratchiness that you get before the record hits the groove is awesome . . . just the ritual of pulling your records out was incredible. You have a stack of a thousand records and you know that three records in from the back was a certain record you wanted to hear. You pull it out of the sleeve, maybe blow the dust off it . . . You set it down all gingerly, you start the arm and wait for it and it's like making a cup of tea or something.

—*SHAWN* ✱✦

LONG-WINDED LEAD-UP

Me and my friends started skating in the summer of '83. BMX culture wasn't doing it for me anymore—every kid and their sister had a Mongoose—so I was open to do something less mainstream and less expensive. Scott Moseley was the first of us to make the switch after Marcus, Frido, and I helped him build a kinky 6-foot quarter-pipe that was too small for our bikes.

A weekend of lawn-mowing could buy you a dusty Kryptonics or Variflex from any number of Bethesda's older brothers who'd been caught up in (and dropped out of) skating's first wave. I got a board off a neighborhood guy in need of a little gas money for his Camaro. It had that clear grip tape embedded with what felt like broken chunks of glass. In hindsight, the *F&R TEAM* graphics on the bottom were prophetic, but they meant nothing to me at the time . . . I just knew it was a huge boat of a board that was way more legit than the skinny warptail knockoff I'd been riding.

Our ramp was tucked behind the abandoned Whalen car dealership next to the Japanese Steak House. We skated it every day, thinking our newfound love of a dead sport was unique. But our short-lived ramp quickly drew in other skaters; loud, dirty guys wearing band shirts I didn't recognize. They skated well and heckled us in a way that was both mocking and supportive: "Don't be a pussy! You can do it! Falling won't hurt as much as me punching you in the fuckin' face if you don't drop in NOW!" These aggressive skate punks turned out to be the not-so-scary Potomac crew of Wiggy, Kenny, Keith, and a young Pete Moffett (then drummer of ENB/Dove, later of G.I.).

That September I entered my freshman year at B-CC High School officially self-identifying as a "skater." Our B-town crew expanded to include Chip Cashel, John Garrish, and Dave Stern (the larval form of Dave Eight). There was this new kid, Richard, in my art class who had transferred from California: hi-top Vans, Mad Rats, short hair, a notebook covered in skate stickers. We struck up a quick friendship so I brought him to the new half-pipe we had just finished in Marcus's back yard.

Before skating, Richard spray-painted band logos all over the ramp: Black Flag, JFA, DOA, Adolescents, Agent Orange, DK's, Circle Jerks. We all agreed it looked pretty cool. When he popped in a tape and played the music for us I was excited by the speed, aggression, and snottiness . . . Seemed like a perfect soundtrack for skating (more so than the Talking Heads). Over the following weeks he lent us tapes, schooled us on hardcore, and even sniffed out a killer local record store called Yesterday & Today.

On one Y&T outing, Dave bought Minor Threat *Out of Step* on a whim and was floored; not just by the music, but by the seemingly unending stream of profanity . . . "This has to be illegal!" he said. The power, precision, and salty language made it stand out over the rest of the bands we had heard. Poring over the cover art, Dave noticed they were from our area, and that's when we realized our town had quite the booming music scene.

In the spring of '84, Richard found out Black Flag was playing D.C. He was relishing his hardcore-curator status, and thought this would be the ideal first show for us. I imagine ours wasn't the only mom-driven station wagon that night to stop in front of Pierce Hall and dump out eight obviously green 13-to-15-year-olds, but I still felt eyeballed. Inside we started to blend into the crowd a bit, taking it all in while huffing the heady mix of cloves, BO, and Rit dye. When local champs Government Issue opened the show, the middle of the old church immediately erupted into a fucking frenzy. Richard quickly coached us on pit etiquette and the finer points of skanking before sending us in like a rookie JV squad.

I wouldn't expect to see Angus Young eating a hot dog at a Journey concert, so I was pretty amazed to see Ian MacKaye there just walking around. It added to the feeling that something was different, where the people who were supposed to be stars or whatever were right there next to you. I heard some guy got beat down in the bathroom, but for the most part people were very cool and friendly . . . everyone just seemed to be going ape shit.

I remember quickly dropping all other music, I remember how much I loved the Faith, how perfect a soundtrack Minor Threat was for skating, how energized I was to be involved in something with my friends that felt new and urgent. It was exciting to realize how expansive this subculture was, to discover that it's going on in my town at that moment. It was like the first look at your haul of Halloween candy spread out across the floor.

I had come in at a time when D.C. hardcore was having some existential growing pains—fucked-up shit that was driving some of its originators out. I didn't know this then because I was part of the problem: an influx of suburban kids jazzed up on slam dancing and stage diving without any sense of the history. The same shows I recall dreamily are recalled with revulsion by others . . . a dumber mutation. Years later I felt the other side of that micro-generational divide—watching new people getting into the scene who were huffing up that same excitement I had lost along the way—feeling like I was surrounded by a bunch of kids in costumes buzzed up on shitty candy.

We moved our half-pipe into a big pocket of woods off Connecticut Avenue and Jones Bridge Road in early 1984. As before, word spread fast through the small network of skaters, with people from our favorite bands showing up at the ramp: Ian (Minor Threat), Eric Lagdameo (Double-O), Bert Queiroz (seemingly every band). Brian Baker (Minor Threat) showed up one day with O.P. Moore from Negative Approach. Watching O.P. do a Miller Flip on our kinky half-pipe is an indelible memory that kinda blew my 14-year-old mind.

Tom Clinton (Youth Brigade, Double-O) had tipped them all off. He worked at the Bethesda Surf Shop where he would kindly answer all my punk and skate questions as he installed my lappers, noserails, and other unnecessary plastic accessories. One day Tom showed up to the ramp with his neighbor Lawrence "the rad" McDonald, a young ripper who had ridden on the skate shop's F&R Team. He'd also seen and/or opened for some of my favorite D.C. bands while playing guitar in his old band, Capital Punishment, with Colin Sears and Mike Fellows. Lawrence and his younger brother Mark were quickly absorbed into our daily skate crew.

The Bethesda Surf Shop (later renamed the Sunshine House, owned by Finnegan & Roberts . . . hence "F&R") was historically significant in the D.C. skate/hardcore scene. Henry Garfield (pre-Rollins), Ian, and Tom had all worked there and rode for the F&R Team over the years. Alec MacKaye (Faith), Bert Q., John Falls (Skewbald), Kenny Inouye (Marginal Man), and others had frequented the shop as well. The shop was near the top of my street in the heart of my hometown (on Cordell Avenue in the same building as WHFS), so it became a daily pit stop for our crew of skaters in '83/'84. Eventually the super-supportive manager Blair Rhodes christened us the next incarnation of the F&R Team. I started working there a year or so later building and selling skateboards, kindly answering questions while adding unnecessary plastic accessories. I think I was 14 or 15.

Our high school had a healthy, goofy punk scene: Natalie Avery and Kate Samworth who would later go on to form Fire Party, Colin and Roger from BMO and later Dag Nasty, Mike Fellows from G.I., Pete Wilborn of the 400, plus nonmusicians Maureen Gorman, Jen Mercurio, Katey Chase, Joel Gwadz, Rob Hardesty, Bill Duvall, Steve Fisher, and others. I feel like being skaters gave us a bit of a late pass with these folks, like, "Oh, how cute! Here come those skaters again." Some of these older punks took a big-brother/sister interest and helped refine our musical tastes. The girls were especially good scene ambassadors; I can't stress this enough . . . they were very enthusiastic in our D.C. musical indoctrination, the recent history, and the newest bands formulating whose smaller, more intimate shows at Food for Thought and community center matinees ran counter to the prevailing scene. One of those new bands was Rites of Spring.

When I saw them for the first time it was clear something else was going on. One by one my friends felt compelled to announce that they would no longer be slam dancing. New bands were influenced by the RoS sound (over, say, G.I.) and named themselves with cryptic prepositional phrases.

Lawrence from my skate crew had started a new band called "Bells of.." with Pete Wilborn (the 400) on drums, Bleu Kopperl on bass, and Alec MacKaye singing. Lawrence asked if I could get my friend Tom Doerr to sit in on drums for a much-needed practice while Pete was off at college . . . In exchange, I could sit in on guitar as well. I imagine that stopgap practice must've felt like a train wreck to Alec, because he quit the band soon after. With a second show already booked, Lawrence officially threw me in the band as second guitar to provide himself cover while he learned how to simultaneously sing and play.

Over the next week or two Lawrence prepared me for the show and took me to buy my first guitar. He told me what kind of strings and pick to get: GHS Boomer 9's and a Jim Dunlop nylon 73—a combination I still use to this day. Through a series of decisions I didn't make, I found myself playing my first show at 15 opening for my two favorite bands, Rites of Spring and Embrace, on October 25, 1985.

After a few more community center shows, Bleu quit and I got shunted over to bass. In early '86 we tracked a 5-song demo at Inner Ear—my first time recording. I was learning a lot from Lawrence (he'd say "stole a lot"), but I lost interest along the way and was replaced by my friend John from our original skate crew. Years later I again had my mind blown when I learned that bass cabinet I had been playing through was Graham McColloch's hand-me-down from Negative Approach—perhaps ditched when the 400 split. To this day I still don't know what the "Bells" were "of.."

I moved back to guitar, increasingly drawn to Metallica's muted rhythmic patterns. The Faith, Minor Threat, and Embrace were also huge influences, making Hampton/Baker/Hetfield my holy trinity. I loved Dag Nasty, too. There were murmurs in the scene that they were a step backwards and a bit too goal-oriented, but I loved hearing their update of a "classic" sound (as if two years was two decades . . . shit was moving fast!).

—JASON †✷❖✣✦❊

REVOLUTION SUMMER

That was a tough time, man, because I felt like I was supposed to really be into all that stuff. It was hard for me to grasp just how ahead of their time Embrace, Rites of Spring, and later Fugazi were . . . because, especially with Embrace, I just wanted to thrash. You listen to those records now and see how progressive they were musically and lyrically. Now that I'm older, I can appreciate it, but back then, man, I was just like, *Fuck this. Fuckin' lame.*

—SHAWN

HOW RAD MALEFICE WAS

I knew Shawn from around: shows; skating; he'd sometimes come into the skate shop where I worked. One day we were at some show talking between bands, probably discussing how rad Malefice was, or comparing skate lines in Riverdale ditch, when he said, "Excuse me, I gotta go now," and jumped straight up on the stage. It dawned on me that he was the singer in Brian Baker's new band. I was surprised and delighted to learn this, and turned to any-some-one to say, "Hey! Shawn is the singer of Dag . . ." but was cut midsentence when Shawn landed on my head in time with their first chord. It made me really mad.

—JASON

OLD COKE

Jason kinda flipped out when Coke changed its formula. I think he bought 20-ish cases of it. A huge stack in the corner of his room. We used to sit there drinking Cokes/playing guitar. We dueled the "Detroit Rock City" lead. It sounded killer, although I know I couldn't play it right.

—DAVE

MY ASS IS HANDED TO ME FOR NOT THE LAST TIME

Washington, D.C., had its share of quirky, trigger-haired skinheads on the set. Eventually I would wise up and learn how to avoid bumping up against them (assisted I imagine by my proximity to Shawn and other folks on the scene who held sway with that demographic), but this wasn't before some scrapes, literal and figurative.

I was a silly and hapless kind of kid, with colorful pants and hair and a faceful of zits, the kind of face that only a mother could love, and the kind of face that could prove tempting to those interested in mopping up the floor with faces.

I could relate many stories, but this one that has really stuck with me because it demonstrates a kind of social logic.

In line at the 9:30 Club on what I believe was the evening D. Boon died, a winter night three days before (or after) Christmas that nonetheless found me and plenty of others in front of the venue, in a T-shirt and light jacket, shivering. Was it the Circle Jerks? No, but I believe it was the very same week. I'm mashing up two evenings, so please forgive me.

Somebody had started a fire either in a garbage can or directly on the ground. This wasn't great for a few reasons, one of which was the cops and/or fire department's disconcerting habit of rolling through punk clubs, looking for excuses to shut everything down. Not a year before, the LAPD had busted up a Black Flag concert at the Palladium in Hollywood and cracked a fair number of skulls, and though it was across country it could have easily been D.C., so we were aware of this dynamic. (Oh, *I* wasn't aware, but others undoubtedly were.)

The squatter's fire was a perfect catalyst for a group of skinheads headed up by the rangy and terrifying Subject 1 to flex. I recall Subject 1 grabbing a grubby dread punk who look approximately like me by the scruff of his neck, the kid who had started the fire . . . Subject 1 screaming in his cowed face that he was out to destroy the scene and fuck shows up for all the innocent citizens just trying to have a good time. Was this what he was doing? The petrified kid assured Subject 1 it was not, which was the only move to make, and after further poking and shaking the guy, Subject 1 lost interest, but he was now activated and righteous in his cause to set posers straight.

I had a Sharpied *X* on my hand, which didn't jibe with the Chicken McNuggets I was busy consuming. My vibe was annoying and I was blissfully unhip to this sad fact. Subject 1 took position in line behind my crew, which my buddies clocked, yet I failed to register. I was loudly analyzing some sort of cartoon that had come with my Happy Meal.

"What is this guy? He looks like a piece of shit. What is he supposed to be?" I said of an abstract cartoon figure. Thinking I was onto something amusing and universal, something that could be shared, I asked of my friends, "Who is this little dude? What's it supposed to be?" They mutely shook their heads, and I, not getting the signal and thinking my wit was worth amplifying, turned to speak to my neighbor at the rear and somehow I registered too late that this was Subject 1, the senior skinhead on the set . . . Indicating the cartoon, I heard myself asking of Subject 1, "What is THIS guy supposed to be?"

The next thing I knew I was reeling, thinking, *What happened? I think I fell*, but no, I was on my feet, reaching up to my forehead which felt wet and cold, my hand coming away bloody.

Subject 1 had plowed me headfirst into the exterior wall of the club. I remember considering the wall, considering the brick. He then twisted my arm behind my back and I nearly fainted.

"IT'S A HUMAN FACE, YOU FAGGOT!"
said Subject 1 through his teeth.
I reckoned he was referring to something else.
I managed a strangled "What . . . ?"

"THE PICTURE, YOU FAGGOT! *WHAT IS IT?*
IT'S A HUMAN FUCKING FACE!"
. . . at which point he left me for dead.

I sat/lay on the curb and my friends, afraid to be associated with the likes of me, waited until the clique of skins was safely in the club to come to my side. Hell, I would've done the same. I had poked the bear, and sadly, lessons were not learned.

Flash forward: was it me walking down the D.C. streets years later? No, I think it was Shawn, or somebody else . . . but I will relate the punch line.

A cop car pulls up alongside Shawn. Shawn or whoever keeps walking, nerves alive and ready to haul ass. The passenger window slides down on the squad car. The driver leans over, hailing Shawn.

It's Subject 1

"Hey," he says, grinning. "Check it out. I'm a cop!"

snare roll/ cymbal catch

—NATHAN

Shawn
Summer 1987
Photo: Ramsey Metcalf

SKINHEADS

It's interesting because I will talk to people about D.C., either people who have visited or are affiliated with D.C., and they bring up, "Oh, the skinheads, the skinheads . . ." and I say, "What about them?You mean to tell me every single skinhead you met in D.C. was a fucking asshole? Every last one? Are you sure about that?"

There are some fucking dicks. I saw some fucking crazy shit, some people got the living shit beat out of them, you know, justly or unjustly. But . . . that's planet earth in general, at least my worldview of it. And really, even though it's not being talked about, the subculture that was there before them was doing the same fucking shit. I mean, like the second show I went to, I think it was Pierce Hall, I saw . . . fuckin' . . . it was Subject 2, Subj. 3 . . . and maybe it was Subj. 4 or somebody like that . . . and Subject 5 beating the living shit out of this dude because he broke the fucking marble partition in the fucking bathroom. I was like . . .

"What the fuck?!"

—SHAWN

STRING

I got my first bass in 9th grade . . . eventually we make plans to start a band called String. Maybe Jason even drew a logo in the vein of the classic *SWIZ*. Could still be somewhere out at 4510. We did have another band before String called Free Admission (like the 5-dollar shows needed to actually be any cheaper in D.C.). F.A. wasn't anything more than a punk H.S. first band. John Garrish played guitar. Not sure who played drums. Fernando Carr? Maybe we never even got that far. String didn't happen. Jason came to me and said Ramsey wanted him for a new thing with Shawn from Dag Nasty.

—*DAVE*

Detail from *Swiz Comic Book*
Fall 1987
Art: Jason Farrell

Chapter 3

GO! *(Swiz with Ramsey)*

TODDLERS WORKING IN TANDEM

Cribbed riffs thru a borrowed amp
sticky fingers
aping and reshaping
till you've made something
you might call your own
then another
and another

In this way
dirty hands get
worked clean

—*JASON*

Ramsey, Positive Force benefit
Johns Hopkins SAIS, Washington, D.C.
July 25, 1987
Photo: Amanda MacKaye

THE BOOK OF RAMSES

1986-87 was mostly golden for me. I had met Shawn a couple years earlier when he was in Dag Nasty through some of our mutual friends, skins from the scene and Master Choy (martial arts community). While playing drums with the Vile Cherubs, I'd hang with Shawn and dream out loud about starting a punk/hardcore project instead of sticking with the Cherubs' '60s-influenced sound. It was the era of side projects—everyone was picking up different instruments and forming new bands. When Shawn suggested we start something new, I jumped at it, choosing guitar over drums. Looking back, I probably should've stuck to drums, since I was gigging fairly regularly and practiced daily. All guitar players want to sit on the drums and vice versa. Its often not a great idea.

My "musical journey" started earlier, back in 6th grade at Georgetown Day School (GDS), playing AC/DC, Ramones, and Kinks covers with Tim Green and assorted classmates. I lived on Cathedral Avenue near MacArthur Boulevard until 8th grade, when we moved to Bethesda. Even after the move, I spent most of my time in D.C., mainly for band practice with Tim and our various projects, including the Cherubs. When my grades slipped to B's and C's in 10th grade, my mom refused to keep paying GDS's steep tuition, so I transferred to Bethesda-Chevy Chase after a brief stint in military school. A big change with new possibilities and temptations abounding.

When Shawn and I started recruiting for the new project, you *(Jason)* were my first pick. I'd heard your very cool "Bells of.." tape, and everyone said you'd fit perfectly. Alex joined next, I think, and then brought in Nathan. We all met at Alex's house one night—my first time meeting Nathan—to discuss forming this "maybe" band or side project.

What I didn't know then was that Seth, Tim, and Jesse had followed me from our Cherubs practice one evening, suspicious about my commitment.

(Left to right)
Tim Green and Ramsey
Circa 1980
Photo: Barbara Jean Metcalf

Their doubts were confirmed when they watched me walk straight into a Swiz rehearsal. I soon left the Cherubs. Tim had grown tired of my moods after three bands together, and while Seth was somewhat upset, they quickly found a great replacement in Ben Wides, a left-handed drummer who played a right-handed setup. (Ben was in several of our previous lineups with me on guitar). Ben went on to become a teacher in NYC, and the Cherubs were his last formal band. The Cherubs thrived and recently rereleased some of their best studio work.

By the early Swiz years, my mom had grown weary of my band life (the basement was both band headquarters at first and too often party central). She'd even stopped relaying the band-practice messages when you guys called, which led to me missing some crucial rehearsals—definitely not helping my situation. My ability to keep current with my high school classwork, work at my job, and attempt to be a good bandmate were undermined by all the usual suspects of an irresponsible teenager. It's truly a minor miracle I graduated on schedule after all the late nights at d.c. space, 9:30 and even schoolnight Baltimore and Richmond adventures. There were multiple killer shows every week, some of which I was up onstage.

The story continues with some interesting historical footnotes, like my connection to Dave Grohl's (maybe first) show with Scream at the Positive Force/Amnesty International gig at Johns Hopkins. I'd made a rookie mistake on our third show's flyer, advertising potential shows with Mission Impossible and 7 Seconds before they were confirmed—typical impulsive 17-year-old move. The 7 Seconds show never materialized beyond some casual talk with Kevin or Dave G., but the M.I. contact led to Dave adding Scream to the lineup for that Amnesty show (which I had helped create and promote). It was a full house and a fantastic show (including King Face and 3). The evening had a humorous end as I headed off with Dave to a party I had been told of in Georgetown. Turns out this was a sorority event and we were anything but the expected guest list, leather-clad and spiky unkempt hair. We were soon approached by the Izod set and asked, "Who are you? Who do you know?" We were shown the door with big grins and a couple of free Dr Peppers. We found the whole episode hilarious. When I recounted the story years later to Dave and his mother Virginia (super nice) and others, we were all howling with laughter. Dave as I recall remarked how much he often misses the anonymity he had back then.

In terms of Hellfire Records, the name had begun as an idea I had while working at Key Bridge Newsstand in Georgetown. Hellfire was to be an after-hours or a speakeasy bar. Shawn was not big on alcohol culture and advised me against opening a bar of any kind. It was an unrealistic idea to start with but great advice from him in retrospect. My involvement with the record label was (extremely) minimal, however I did try to sell some of the first single, which I eventually returned (the last 15 copies) to you last year!! What other record label takes returns after 30 years?

Recording our demo at Inner Ear with Don Zientara was a highlight, despite my underwhelming mini "solo." Don offered to let us rerecord parts, but as everyone knows: Time = Money, and we never returned to rework or master. Overall it's a solid recording for a demo. We managed to land that first 9:30 Club show with the Adolescents thanks to some legwork I did delivering this demo tape (though Shawn's reputation probably sealed the deal). By the time the show happened, I was unfortunately out of the band.

Looking back, I'm proud to have been part of all of your musical careers, even though my ambitions outpaced my skills and work ethic at that point in my life. We played some epic shows during my time, and I'm at peace with my contribution. I do sometimes wonder if buying that Italian motorcycle instead of a better Marshall stack (or was it an SG to replace my twangy Rickenbacker?) was the right call. I guess I was running from reality back then.

—***RAMSEY*** *(in correspondence with Jason)*

DAY 1

I was working at Moto Foto in the early spring of 1987 when Shawn walked in. I hadn't met the kid he brought with him: a Mod who had transferred to my high school earlier that same year. Shawn introduced him as Ramsey and declared their intentions of staring a new band in the vein of Bad Brains. They were assembling members and were wondering if I'd want to play guitar along with Ramsey. Having been ousted from Bells of.. a year prior and eager to play again, I said yes. They had no film to process so there was not much more to discuss. The whole exchange took about three minutes.

I told Dave about it when he got back from lunch or whatever, and he was psyched. He wanted to know if there was room for him as another guitar, but with Ramsey claiming first chair it was not an option.

Some days later, in April 1987, I borrowed a Marshall head from my friend John (the guy who replaced me in Bells of..) to meet Shawn and Ramsey at Ramsey's house for the first practice. Turns out he lived in my neighborhood, but the far end . . . too far to roll an amp. I borrowed my dad's Porsche and crammed my borrowed shit into it to drive the 8 blocks. Two other young men were recruited for the rhythm section: drummer Alex Daniels from nearby Tulip Hill and bassist Nathan Larson from Capitol Hill in D.C. proper. We set up in what must've been a rumpus room off the living room on the ground floor; a wholly un-soundproofed and doorless area. Ramsey's mom stopped us midsong to let us know we sounded horrible, then stopped herself midsentence to say, "Y'all smell like a pack of lizards!"

I strongly disagreed with the former . . . couldn't defend the latter.

—JASON

BIG DREAMS

Ramsey had a lot of big dreams for the band.
He said he could get us a spot opening for the Bad Brains.
This all made me really excited . . .
the prospect that we could play shows
with an audience.

—*ALEX*

LIES

There's many ups downs, in outs, round a rounds, gettin' to a finished song Jason was working on the riff for "Lie" and I was trying to figure out some AC/DC song. We were both in his room playing guitar. This is debatable. It's also a fun in my brain. I think he thought I was trying to help him with his song so he grabbed my wrong AC/DC chords for the chorus to "Lie."

We all remember stuff differently. Jason can remember how to play shit we did in our 20s and lyrics off a random Didgits record we haven't heard in as much time. I can't remember where I was on-set shooting yesterday.

—*DAVE*

REJECTS (SPRING 1987)

Pack of Lizards

The Forgiven

The Unforgiven

Noble Creon

Battery

—*SWIZ*

THE ALMIGHTY . . .

When all is said and done, let's face it: "Swiz" is the best name ever used by a rock band. Short. To the point. Has a "z." What more could you ask for? It isn't an acronym, a surefire way to fade into obscurity. It isn't a phrase that gives the listener too much to think about (sorry, Rain Like the Sound of Trains and One Last Wish). It's a jab. Or maybe a slash.

And on top of all of that, even having already established how great the name is . . . it has literary origins and social commentary packed into its four letters. A swiz, British slang for a swindle, evoking the Sex Pistols, wasted energy on popular culture, and a story about a liminal equine arsonist all in one fell swoop.

Every band I've played in since has had to come up with a name.
Each time, each suggestion:
"It's no Swiz."

—*ALEX*

SCARY LOGO

I came to one practice with *Swiz* written all over my Peavey cabinet, all these different ways . . . a 4x12 flash sheet of logos. One bit the KISS lightning bolts, another ripped off the Monkees as an SG silhouette. The dumbest was a tipped-over jar with *swiz* dripping out. The "scary" logo won hands down. It was a style of lettering I had been messing around with for about a year, equal parts Misfits and Minor Threat. Funny how a precise outline can make any mess look deliberate. Alex asked me to replace the "x" that originally dotted the "i" for a regular (but still scary) dot so no one mistook us for "edge."

I'd draw it straight on acetate with a rapidograph pen to make a shirt screen, then redraw it again for each show flyer . . . I probably drew it a hundred times before it was pointed out to me that I could simply Xerox the best one. But I'm glad I didn't know that trick . . . I like how the logo morphed over time.

—JASON

Proposed logos
Spring 1987
Art: Jason Farrell

BLACK FLAG

I was definitely one who really wanted to evoke that strange feeling you get sometimes when you're listening to Black Flag.

They were one band who would make me feel weird . . . There is such a mood and atmosphere that music created that I still can't describe, and that was something I was always trying to tap into, something I was really trying to get across.

I wanted to do that in Swiz.

—SHAWN 

ROLLINS

I once interviewed Henry Rollins at my college radio station. I asked him: "What does the new record sound like?"

Without skipping a beat, he said, "It sounds like me picking you up and throwing you out the window." (We were on the fifth floor.) I liked this description—it made a real impression on me!

I think the sound we were looking for in Swiz was angry and brutal, but that's not all I felt while playing. I felt uplifted during the choruses, and like I was issuing a call for action when I struck the bell of the ride cymbal with the shank of my drumstick. Every time I pounded away on the snare drum on the two and four, I was socking it to my worst demon, and I was totally faking you out of your shorts when I tried to syncopate a rhythm on the bass drum.

So, in other words, I wasn't really thinking, *This is the sound I want to play/band I want to be in.* I was really into the physicality of playing. The drumbeat and coordination with the other band members had to envelop everything and it was really, really, really important. Without subtlety. So, yes, like me throwing you out the window. BUT MORE.

—*ALEX*

QUALIFIED FOR THAT

It looked fierce worn low, to the knees if possible. Moreover, it looked more manageable than a regular guitar. It's longer, but it's got two less strings to worry about. Dee Dee Ramone said: "1, 2, 3, 4." Consider the cover of the Clash's *London Calling*, that's a bass Paul Simonon is about to smash. I can't think of a single image that spoke to me more, and I know this particular photo had a far-reaching effect on many folks. I wanted to:

1) Be punk and skinny like that guy . . . or,

2) Failing that, get the chance to smash something . . . I felt qualified for that.

Another advantage was as a bass player, you have the option of stepping forward and making yourself seen, or you can hide back in the half dark back by your amp. And you could suck ass—nobody really cares what you played, you could play bad and it would matter a lot less than, say, sucking ass on the drums, which is quite conspicuous in comparison.

To sum up: if you sucked on the bass (see Sid Vicious), you had better (as mentioned) be skinny and hot . . . and I was, in fact, neither. The outside option was to just be crazy and jump around, so I aimed for that modality in Swiz but never quite got all the way there.

—NATHAN

I MEAN, DID I EVER REALLY FEEL COMFORTABLE?

I think at the time just having been the singer of Dag Nasty and just gone through all that fucking shit . . . and having put a bunch of shit on myself that I realize now that I'm older, it's like, *Why did you put that shit on yourself?*

I always saw the potential of Swiz, but going back to that first demo, I think that it was so different at the time that I got intimidated a little bit and wasn't really sure what to do with it myself. I really had to kind of let go or just trust myself and what was going on in order for that to even happen, you know what I mean? Because there's a lot of internal self-judgment or, just like . . . trying to live up to what I thought the sound should be.

If you do something and you have some success and you like what you're doing or whatever, sometimes the tendency is to stick to the same formula or something that was similar to it. But that also can be what sinks you, which I kind of realized, you know . . . maybe not in the beginning, but . . . early on. And also the fact that the band needed to grow. We had to cycle through a bunch of the songs that we played in the beginning in order to write the stuff that we were writing later on.

—*SHAWN*

HONOR RO

@ D.C. SPACE

June 25th

MCMLXXXVII

JUNE 25, 1987

Swiz played its first show
at d.c. space opening for Honor Role.
I don't remember much about it, beyond
drinking countless Jolt Colas to get amped
which only left me crazy jittery.

We played 8 songs—a number
that would become our standard.
Count the collective 5 minutes
of sporadic/inexpert tuning and
we may have eked out a 20-minute set.

—JASON

Previous spread:
Show flyer, first show, original art
June 25, 1987
Art: Jason Farrell

STAR-CROSSED

It was "beach week," a time when rich kids converge on the DelMarVa shore to party after school lets out. I was in the middle of making the decision to stay in D.C. instead of starting my freshman year at NYU. Part of me knew that New York would probably eat me alive. I was at least self-aware enough to realize that. But it wasn't just the fear of trying something new that kept me in D.C. I decided to stay because I had somehow landed smack in the middle of a group of people who all seemed to agree that things were feeling right.

Around midweek, I was lying on the beach at dusk zoning out and someone says, "So-and so's been looking for you."

We eventually met up and lay down on our backs in the sand, looking up at the nighttime sky. I saw a shooting star. That summer I practiced as much as I could, spent time with her as much as I could, sneaking out of her house in the wee hours, and sleepwalking through my temp job as a file clerk downtown.

Playing in Swiz coincided with my first love. At our first show, I got off the stage and got a big hug. Later that night, after swimming in a friend's pool, our first kiss. My first kiss . . . I mean, the first one that meant something anyway.

Over the next few years, it was hard to keep the band, school, and the relationship together. Maybe the shooting star, a cosmic sign at the beginning of the relationship, caused me to hold on to it far longer than I should have.

In the end, although it took me a long time to accept that it was the case, I chose the band over the relationship. Either way, neither one was really meant to last. And in each case, I wish the end was a little different, that I had made a cleaner break and stopped looking back. Growing up is hard that way.

—ALEX

HEY, KIDS!
A MATINEE SHOW
FEATURING...
THE MOTIVES
IGNITION
AT THE
HUNG JURY PUB
THE SILENCE AFTER
SWIZ
JUNE 28th
JASON

JUNE 28, 1987

Just 3 days after our first show, we loaded in to the Hung Jury Pub in D.C. for our second; a Sunday matinee with fellow D.C. bands Ignition, the Motives, and the Silence After. I remember nothing about our set or theirs, but two memories are stuck in my mind surrounding the whole event.

One was watching Ignition function in the space: the way they carried themselves, set up their equipment . . . they looked like they knew what they were doing—a sharp contrast to how the other less-experienced bands were milling around (e.g., Swiz). Chris Bald had an army duffel bag or something with fresh copies of their then-new first 7", like he had just hiked the Appalachian Trail back from the pressing plant. I bought it . . . still have it. I noticed all this because I was watching them pretty closely through side glances. The Faith was (and is) my favorite band, but I never got to see them (having only found out about the punk rocks just months after their demise), so I was fully primed to like any new band with Faith members. When Rites of Spring and Embrace played I was there as often as my schedule as a 15-year-old would allow. But of all the D.C. bands I've gotten to see, Ignition looms largest in my mind . . . partly for the Faith lineage which they carried well . . . but more for the work ethic, the lyrics, the songs, Alec's voice/presence, the moments that felt like everything was on the verge of falling apart, and the moments everything did. Watching them through their couple years, I witnessed more rare moments of spooky transcendence onstage (and well past those confines) than any other band I've seen.

The second memory is drawing the show flyer while sitting at my grampa's kitchen table. At 17, I was still taking trips with my family to visit him in Dushore, Pennsylvania, a small, hilly town whose main intersection had a Ben Franklin 5 & dime, the town's sole public phone booth, and the only traffic light in Sullivan County. Grampa had been living in a small ground-floor 1-bedroom apartment a half-block down from that phone booth which served as our primary means of communicating with him. His place was dark. I recall just one window—by the front door—the blue sunlight barely made it midway through the apartment to the kitchen where I drew under warm incandescents. He smiled a lot and had a good laugh, like his son.

—JASON

Show flyer
June 28, 1987
Art: Jason Farrell

Show flyer
July 18, 1987
Design: Ramsey Metcalf

JULY 18, 1987

d.c. space was a was small, intimate room with a low stage. What it might have lacked in sound quality it made up for tenfold in being an amazing social hub: lots of chatting, flirting, joking . . . a very happy/social/fun vibe. We got there before Soulside, and Ramsey took it upon himself to start running the door. He set a door price of 4 bucks, which seemed like a fair price to all of us . . . I can't remember if that was the exact amount, but I do remember it was quickly deemed $1 too much by Soulside when they finally got there, causing a bit of a mini-panic. After a quick damage-control assessment, the big kids took over. Ramsey was shunted off door duty, and the politically/socially acceptable amount of one-dollar-less was reinstated. Did I see singles being hastily redistributed to those already in the venue? . . . Can't be sure. It's my first recollection of some underlying politics or rules attached to being in a band in D.C.—etiquette we were expected to already know or at least learn fast. It was not the last time we would fail in that regard.

—JASON

Show flyer
July 18, 1987
Art: Soulside

Swiz, d.c. space
July 18, 1987
Photo: Ethan Minsker

Jason and Shawn, *Down* photo shoot #1, Great Falls, MD
July 22, 1987
Photos: Ramsey Metcalf

OUT ON THE WARM ROCKS

tired from climbing
that good sick feeling
of water in my nose
and snot to spit

sat on the cliff
we don't talk about relationships
of sun, gravity, and river
how passing from wet to dry
is like slow breathing
just trivial things

I wait to want to move
Ben watches the current below
this liminal moment feels like always
till summer wins over
and I'm hot again, breath caught
for one last jump, three hard steps then
nothing

the walk back is silent save for our low-tops squishing,
coarse river sand drying in my hair

—JASON

JULY 25, 1987

The Johns Hopkins U show was our first of many Positive Force benefits, this one for Amnesty International. Don't remember much, except that Nathan, Shawn and Alex wore matching smiley face shirts . . . and that Alex was very impressed with Scream's new drummer . . . and that 3 had Jeff Nelson in it, so I probably watched them closely. I loved King Face, and I'm sure they killed it as per usual, but seeing them in fluorescent overhead lighting with the afternoon sunlight streaming through the windows was a bit of a disconnect. Their sexy-rock powers couldn't be fully realized until after nightfall.

After the show everyone was supposed to grab candles and march past the nearby embassies in protest of human rights violations. Being a new band, we hadn't yet learned that you pack your shit up as fast as you can immediately after you play. So as all the boys and girls and more seasoned bands started marching into the evening light down Mass. Ave., I was looking at a jumble of Swiz crap spread out around the back wall.

By the time we packed up our stuff, the protest was long since done. I imagined all the boys/girls/seasoned bands were marching off to whatever party that night may have offered. I was bummed to have missed both.

—JASON

AUGUST 7, 1987

Far more notable than the numerical distinction of this being show #5 was the fact that it was our last show as a five-piece, and our hands-down worst show ever.

A few days prior, the rest of us let Ramsey know we wanted him to leave Swiz. He had started the band with Shawn, sought out the members to complete it (Alex, Nathan, and me), wrote riffs for some of our earliest songs ("Much," "Memory") as well as lyrics ("Taste," "Condemn," "Reach") . . . so he was a bit blindsided by the coup. As the external presentation of our band developed through practices and early shows, we internally jockeyed for position and influence, each hoping to shape the direction the band would take.

Despite Ramsey's contributions, he was often at odds with the vision that was gelling between the rest of us, and his de facto leader status (which is always tenuous between teenagers) quickly eroded. Though the ousting was presented as "effective immediately," Ramsey asked to stay on for that last show.

The rest of us were feeling pretty cocky having powered through 4 strong shows thus far. We were to play in Virginia with Nathan's close friends Shudder to Think, along with Injury, Blackout and New Carrollton at the Lee Center: a sort of community space with no stage and not much of a sound system. This would prove to be a problem.

As we started our set, none of us could hear each other. We lacked any real experience to draw on with this sort of challenge. Things quickly fell out of sync, then totally fell apart. We had to stop no less than three songs due to being completely lost. The middle of our set could be summed up as awkward silence punctuated by fractions of songs.

Show flyer
July 25, 1987
Courtesy of Positive Force

After the third failing, Alex picked up the chair that was serving as his stick holder and threw it across the room in frustration, spreading his backup sticks far away across the back wall. A song or two later when he had broken the sticks in his hands, he had to sheepishly walk back to pick up replacements.

I imagine that the goodwill and leeway most people are willing to extend to an up-and-coming band were exhausted on that day. Thankfully, with the public humbling came some focus . . . We managed to get a little better.

Swiz was hugely in debt to Ramsey, without whom we would have never banded. But the decision to kick out a cofounder, though hard, looked clear and necessary. And who better than 17-year-olds to carry out cutthroat acts of self-interest?

—JASON

MY MAIN THING

Our parting ways with Ramsey reflected the real bond the other members had with one another. That's the truth. But it doesn't make the fact that a bunch of teenagers kicked their friend out of a band any nicer—especially when Ramsey hadn't actually done anything "wrong."

I think parting with Ramsey—and the fact that I decided to stay in D.C. for college, rather than go the New York as originally planned—made the band a lot more serious for me. Not like a job serious, but like a reason for being. I still did "life" . . . but the band was my main thing.

—ALEX

Show flyer, last show with Ramsey, original art
August 7, 1987
Art: Jason Farrell

8/7/87
SWIZ
@
THE
LEE
CENTER
ACROSS CHAIN BRIDGE,
Injury
Blackout
Shudder to Think
New Carrolton

Chapter 4

LEAN

(Down to fighting weight)

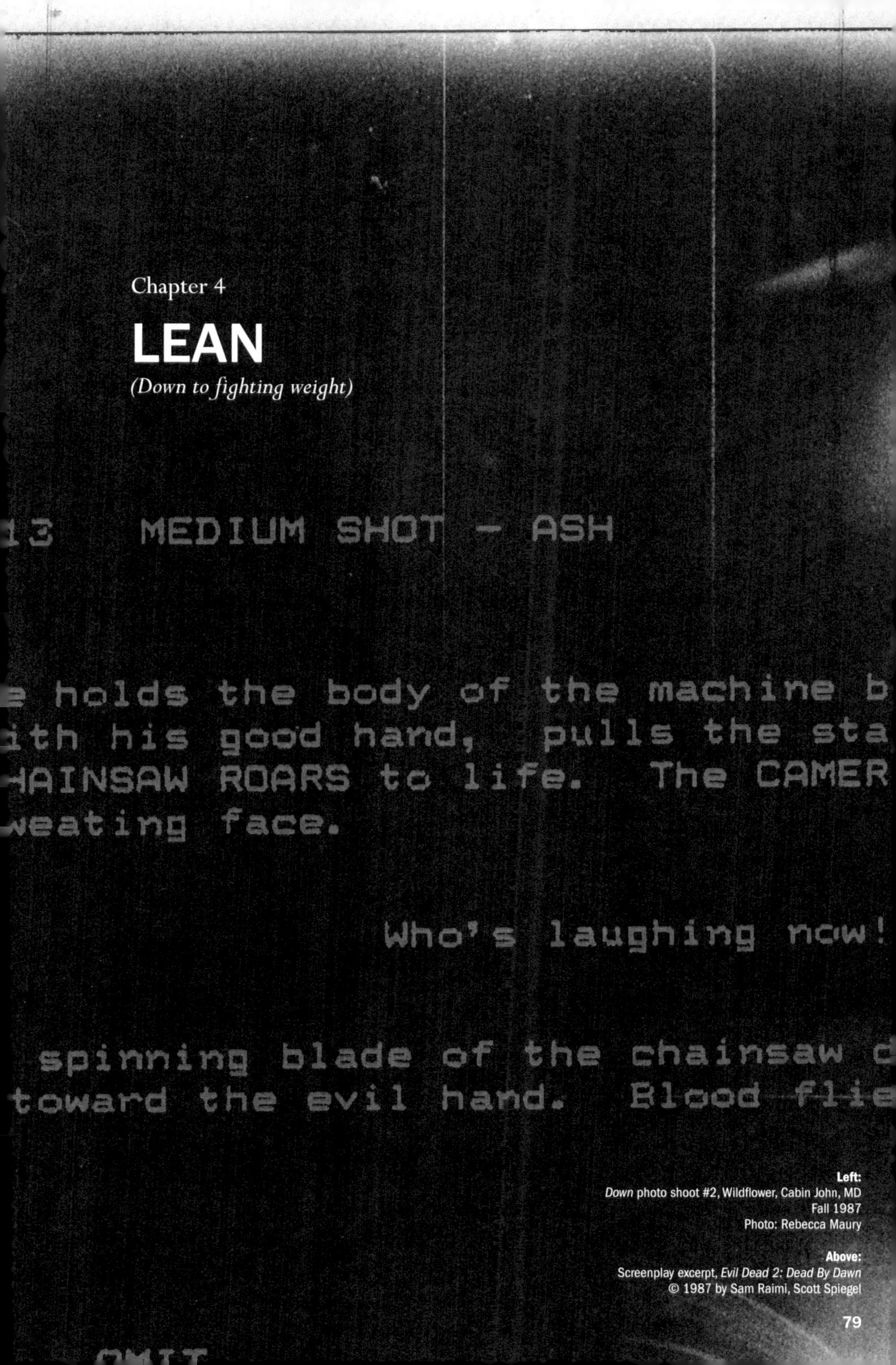

13 MEDIUM SHOT - ASH

e holds the body of the machine b
ith his good hand, pulls the sta
HAINSAW ROARS to life. The CAMER
weating face.

Who's laughing now!

spinning blade of the chainsaw d
toward the evil hand. Blood flie

Left:
Down photo shoot #2, Wildflower, Cabin John, MD
Fall 1987
Photo: Rebecca Maury

Above:
Screenplay excerpt, *Evil Dead 2: Dead By Dawn*
© 1987 by Sam Raimi, Scott Spiegel

9:30 CLUB
ADOLE-
SCENTS
SWIZ
YOUTH OF
TODAY
SEPTEMBER 9th
9:30 CLUB... 9th & F STREETS

I WAS STOKED, MAN

I couldn't even believe it.
Man, I'm gonna meet Tony Cadena!

—*SHAWN*

SEPTEMBER 9, 1987 *(Adolescents, Youth of Today, Swiz at the 9:30 Club)*

Our first show without cofounder and coguitarist Ramsey, having asked him to leave a month before. It was also our first show at a proper/legit venue—the 9:30 Club. Alex, Nathan, Shawn, and I practiced like mad to be up to speed, hoping to wash away the memory of having shit our diapers at the Lee Center show. Maybe it was lingering apprehension that led us to debate ways we could spice up the set. Not sure how we landed on renting a smoke machine, nor why the others agreed to letting me start the show with a "blistering" solo (I had just learned how to do hammer-ons . . . barely), but one smoky/wonky lead and a few scratching heads later, we were plowing through our first set as a stripped-down 4-piece.

I hadn't heard Youth of Today at that point, and was only marginally aware of the budding straight edge scene that would steamroll the US hardcore landscape in a few short months. J. J. Wilcoxon, a young sXe enthusiast we knew (and cousin to my friend Marcus), showed us the newest dance craze we were likely to see that evening. He said it was called "moshing" and it looked just as cool and innovative then as it does today.

Four years earlier, the Adolescents were among the first punk/HC bands I had ever heard, part of a package deal of Cali HC bands that our friend Richard Basch had exposed us to (T.S.O.L, RF7, the Faction, Circle Jerks, etc. . . . the skate-punk starter kit for 13-year-olds). But by '87, my head was so far up the ass of D.C. that I had no connection as I watched their set. I kick myself now for not having appreciated the opportunity/honor of playing with such a great band.

—*JASON*

Show flyer, first show as a 4-piece
September 9, 1987
Art: Jason Farrell

MR. NO-SHOW

During the first year of the band, Nathan and I worked at a movie theater in Northwest D.C. I had worked in movie theaters throughout high school thanks to a connection I had with two brothers who owned the Circle Theater chain in the city—they went to the same church that I did. In high school, the theater where I worked, which is now a restaurant about 100 yards down the street from the newsroom where I work, was mostly staffed by people with connections to the Bangladeshi embassy. Lots of ushers driving Mercedes with diplomatic plates . . .

But ownership had changed when Nathan and I got the jobs, and we were at a brand-new movie theater way uptown. This one was managed by a guy who would not let me drift from my ticket-taker post 15 feet over to Nathan's popcorn stand in between movies to talk. I think his expectation was that I should be like a Buckingham Palace guard, and remain rigid and stone-faced.

For a while, maybe a month, it worked out. My life was school, movie theater, and band practice—we'd get together twice a week. Finally the movie theater became pretty annoying and I just stopped showing up. But I hadn't gotten paid. After putting it off for a while, I marched in and asked for my check.

"Ah, Mr. No-Show," came the manager's greeting when I was shown into his office.

—ALEX

SWEET SIXTEEN(-ISH) *(September 12 or thereabouts, 1987 Shudder to Think and Swiz at d.c. space)*

We had to come up with some half-assed excuse to drag a distracted and pissy Nathan down to d.c. space on a sunny Saturday afternoon for his . . . SURPRISE SWEET 16 BIRTHDAY PARTY!!!! As we ushered him through the door, Nathan's favorite band, Shudder To Think, started playing (probably some swank-ified happy b-day song) and the irritated confusion on Nate's face melted into sheer bliss. Smiling ear to ear, he floated through the crowd of fresh young well-wishers, eventually landing on the side of the stage with a slapping tambourine in his hand—his first performance with his future band (at least that's how I remember it). Our little boy was a man. A driver's license was issued posthaste, followed a few months later by the blue Chevy van that would whisk us across the country.

Oh shit! My bad . . . it was Nathan's 17th birthday, not 16 . . . but no less sweet. Apparently all organized by his crazy-supportive mom and dad (who, coincidentally, hooked him up with said blue van).

Already a legal driver, too, so . . . whatever . . .

It was a long time ago.

—*JASON*

CARVE OUT YOUR OWN SHIT *(a conversation)*

[00:47:12] Speaker 1: "I saw this weird class thing when people sort of pass judgment on the Dupont Circle 'drunk punk' scene. There were either people there that were in that lifestyle to escape from or cope with what life gave them, or people who came from money and were trying to emulate that lifestyle. But there are also people that were on, I think, the more art-scene-controlling end. For a kid that runs away from maybe Vermont and goes to live on the street in D.C., there's a kid in D.C. who maybe hangs out and is living a lifestyle that's not approved by his parents, only later to become, like, a world-famous actor or painter. So *that's* OK . . . you know what I mean? Like, 'We're going to let you have your crazy years.' But that same art kid is making a judgment on that other street kid who's trying to figure out what he's doing . . . or she's doing." *[00:47:59][47.1]*

[00:48:00] Speaker 2: "It's a Shakespeare story . . . I haven't read it, but it's basically, like, 'I'm going to slum it till my trust fund comes in.'" *(Henry IV, Part I, II) [00:48:15][14.6]*

[00:48:15] Speaker 1: "Oh, man . . . D.C.! You and I both know, to this day, we both know motherfuckers are just always destined to be rich and comfortable . . . by birth. And that's OK, you know. I love my brother Subject 6 I love him. I do. He landed where he landed in life as far as like being brought on the planet earth, you know what I mean? But that was always going to be that guy's trajectory. Always. Which is interesting when you think about it because . . . I think about bands and music and stuff with him as truly being like a hobby. You know, I look back at that whole time, and it's like, *Oh, he's just . . . he's whittling . . . maybe he'll be able to, like, sell some of those whittlings*. But, you know, just . . . whittling along. *[00:49:26][46.1]*

[00:49:27] Speaker 2: "Those are some damn good whittles, though. I love Band 1 *[00:49:29][2.6]*

[00:49:30] Speaker 1: "I love him. Like I said, not taking anything from him or disrespect or anything like that. Subject 7 is another one who's just . . . you know, 'I'm still doing my hobby.'" *[00:49:48][18.5]*

[00:49:49] Speaker 2: "Yeah, I remember some conversation with Subj. 8 where he was talking about that kind of dynamic . . . not being able to fully trust someone who never had and never needed a job. Like, can we even see things the same? It's kind of hard *not* to be suspicious of someone who is living on that golden pillow or whatever, you know what I mean?" *[00:50:20][30.4]*

[00:50:21] Speaker 1: "Yes . . . 'These punk kids are fun, but . . .'" *[00:50:25][4.3]*

[00:50:27] Speaker 2: "Cue exit! (Ha ha.) Shit, man, but fuck, I'm so glad that he wrote and continues to write music—Band 2, Band 3—two of my favorite bands." *[00:50:32][5.8]*

[00:50:33] Speaker 1: "Yeah! And there's heart in that shit too, you know what I mean? There's a lot of heart. It's just, you know, people approach things differently, express things differently.

"I say this real quick: You are still the first person, the only person, I could really relate to at that time, because your world was a lot like mine, you know, you had like the same type of family structure. Not exactly the same, but you were living in a house with multiple people and everything wasn't marble and fucking shiny. Your parents are real working fucking people. You know, you had real fucking issues. You know I love Subject 9, but it wasn't like going over to his house and his mom saying, 'I made you some lemonade, now get out of my hair, I'm busy fucking picking jewelry,' or whatever she was doing, and Dad is coming home from some serious professional jobs and money and they had these lifestyles already set up, you know what I mean?

"Going out to D.C., I'd go to some party in Georgetown and think, *What the fuck is this?!* To this day, I still remember that was a real revelation, something I really noticed because I was just always like, *Does everyone down here live this lifestyle?*

"I feel like that for cats like us, for better or worse or whatever, you had to carve out your own shit, you know. That's kind of what I appreciated about the MacKayes as well . . . slightly different circumstances, but just that type of reality. I mean, because that guy . . . you know, despite what anybody says about him, Ian made his life for himself. I mean, thinking of 'Fuck it, I'm not going to college' and just focusing on some fucking dumb subculture lifestyle that you're living . . . and then making something out of it. When you think about it back in the day, that's a ballsy-ass fucking thing to do. It's wild that he fucking pulled it off.

"Another really wild thing, I was looking at some old pictures of the guy the other day, just kind of looking at the whole evolution of that man through these different pictures. You see a look on his face . . . I just remember where his personality was at the time, you know, very, like, smart and fucking like . . . not conniving, but just planning." *[00:52:32] [119.7]*

[00:52:33] Speaker 2: "Always alert. It was very much like, 'I'm up here, I'm in control, I'm going to control the situation. I'm going to play this music and you're going to enjoy it or you're not going to enjoy it, but you're not going to fuck it up.' I mean, it was watching control happening, which in and of itself was really . . . alluring. My god, when I think of Alec and Ignition, it was the opposite, like watching some snake handler go off in a trance, losing control and just giving himself up willingly to the moment . . . it was amazing. Ian was very much not that at all. Interesting contrast, when you see two people, singers, brothers . . . one pure control, the other total abandon.

"Going back to Subject 6, I kept waiting for him to *not* be so nice. So 'Yeah, that's great, Jason! Good for you!' So fucking supportive that you're kind of waiting for the sarcastic eye roll . . . and it never comes. My whole training as a kid was to be a little bit mistrustful of people because *anybody* might be fucking with you mentally or physically. It was just how kids I knew interacted, like that was the social currency. So you had to be 'on' . . . suspicious, ready with defenses and preemptive offenses to avoid being on the losing end of these weird competitive exchanges, right? But he is, like, genuinely so fucking nice . . . and he never drops it. Never. I've never seen him, like, angry or mean." *[00:54:09][96.1]*

[00:54:10] Speaker 1: "I've never seen him angry or mean either." *[00:54:13][3.1]*

[00:54:14] Speaker 2: "Yeah, and I'm not saying he can't be sad. But I'm saying, like, at some point I had to tweak my worldview and accept that there are people who are just . . . they're just nice. And they're not trying to get anything from you. He doesn't need anything from me. He's got all he needs." *[00:55:31][17.2]*

[00:55:32] Speaker 1: "That's why probably—I'm not saying it manifest in everybody like that, but—that's probably part of it. I mean, if you realize, *Why would I be a dick? Maybe I just invite these bums over to my fucking house to hang out and watch a movie and have my parents fucking feed them and bring, like, hot girls over and we can have beer.* You know? I mean, his place, his parents' house, was a spot for weekends, man." *[00:57:04][31.5]*

# # #

—**SHAWN** (Speaker 1) / **JASON** (Speaker 2)

·DARKNESS -AT- NOON·

September 26th

St. Stephens Episcopal †
Church

2 blocks from
Wilson Center
off 16th STREET

a POSITIVE FORCE SPONSORED
BENEFIT

SEPTEMBER 26, 1987 *(Darkness at Noon, Fugazi, Sarcastic Orgasm, Swiz at St. Stephen's Church)*

This was the 8th show for Swiz, and our second Positive Force event—a benefit concert for a gay and lesbian march in D.C. The enthusiasm in D.C. for "Ian's new band" was high, and we were honored to be on the bill. I hoped our stabs at a vintage DCHC sound weren't going to be seen as something to suffer through while waiting for Fugazi to start. Thankfully, we were starting to get some interest of our own. One faction of support was from kids still hopped up on *The Age of Quarrel*, so there may have been a brief moment of slam dancing during a particularly moshy part of our set (generally frowned upon at a Positive Force event).

The most notable historic tidbit about this show is that it was Fugazi's second live performance and—if legend and rumor are to be believed—Guy's first with the band. I can't remember well enough to verify this, nor can I find photographic evidence to confirm my own questionable memory of Ian having a long mop of curly hair at the time . . . I don't even remember much of Darkness at Noon or the Swiz sets . . . but I *can* vividly recall the two shirtless onstage dancer dudes in sparkly hot pants air-humping their way through Sarcastic Orgasm. And I remember that it triggered some dark responses from the more macho element of the crowd.

Shows were the hub of a large and loose social circle. A wide range of ages and interests that weren't necessarily in sync could be found at any given event. A few came to fight, others to fuck, while the rest of these 15-25-year-olds were simply there to engage with their friends and listen to music.

Most of the kids at the shows were aligned with (or at least open to learning about) the causes Positive Force championed. But even in a scene known for having a progressive/active stance on social issues, 30+ years ago there were still people hovering somewhere between ambivalence, discomfort, and hostility when it came to LGBTQ rights.

Show flyer
September 26, 1987
Art: Jason Farrell

Sure . . . watching stage dancers thrusting hyper-sexualized gestures can make people feel uncomfortable (gay or straight, joking or serious). But even with that in mind, I was surprised by some of the reactions and comments we heard later: people being disappointed that we would play a "gay show" with a "gay band" like that, how far we'd fallen or whatever. These comments sounded as stupid as they were, and started to distance us from some of the people who liked our band. It made me question what we were doing musically to attract the kind of people who couldn't deal with something as ridiculous as Sarcastic Orgasm—they were funny . . . the name is awesome . . . I don't remember if they were any good, but still, if you felt uncomfortable you could just go outside till Fugazi came on.

Shawn was never one to shy away from this issue. During one show he asked a heckler, "What if I *am* gay? Does it matter? How would it change anything?" I remember talking to Shawn after the show, saying something like, "That was a good speech, but you didn't tell them you *weren't* gay . . . now they might think you are."

He said, "So what?"

At 17, I was still a ways from having the sense or confidence or heart to make the same statement.

—JASON

"SAY HEY TO YOUR FRIEND SPIDER FOR ME!" *(Paul "Snowshoes" Dever's brother)*

He never wrote a song. Didn't know Dolby from MIDI.
But somehow Paul knew how to sneak a little "Shazam" into the mix.

I met my road-trip-driving,
show-going,
Tastee Diner-eating
buddy during my first week at Catholic University.

Introducing myself was easy . . .

"Hello," I said as I approached him one evening on campus.
"I notice you have *Dag Nasty* written on your shoe."

—*ALEX*

MUCH TIME CAUSE LIE

In October of 1987, Swiz went to Inner Ear Studio to record songs for our debut 7". Back then, Don Zientara's legendary studio had all the trappings of the basement it was: laundry machine, furnace, kid toys, etc. We set up amps and drums in the main room with homemade baffles separating the instruments. Shawn holed up in the laundry closet with a vocal mic. The small control room, woven with house duct work, held a legit 16-track plus a mess of puzzles and such to keep fidgety band members occupied. Despite what sounds like a humble setting, I was incredibly honored and psyched to be recording—and to simply *be*—in the place where my favorite records were captured. In bold red and black marker, rows of white tape boxes bore the names of the bands that had come before us . . . *Faith, Minor Threat, Rites of Spring* . . . all in Don's loopy handwriting.

Don is a super-nice, super-tall dude who looked even taller when tucked under the low basement ceiling (. . . and tucked into tennis shorts that made his already-long legs seem impossibly longer). We assumed Don would be working the machines start to finish like he had on our demo a few months prior, but midsession he ducked out (literally) and a young Eli Janney bounded in. Though I was a bit nervous to have him cut his teeth on our tape, Eli ended up being a good fit and he would go on to record all the Swiz sessions over the years that followed.

We were well-practiced from all the shows of late, so my recollection is that things went smoothly/quickly. Shawn and Eli's buddy Bobby Sullivan (Soulside) swung by for a bit, lending some backup vocals. We tracked 6 songs that day, mixed the four we thought sounded the toughest ("Much," "Time," "Cause," "Lie"), and left the other two softies on the reel ("Sorry" and "Slide," released posthumously by THD Records as the *Rejects* 7").

I had suggested the title *Down* since all the songs had that word as a lyric. But *Down* was also the name of a song from my previous band Bells of.., and the cliff-jumping shot on our back cover was a concept Bells of.. leader Lawrence had planned to someday use for his debut . . . and the opening riff to "Lie" bore a striking resemblance to a Bells of.. song called "Amounts."

All these coincidences looked like grand theft to Lawrence, and made for years of icy awkward moments at the skate ramp. I could refute each claim ("down" is a cool-sounding word no one owns, that was *not* Lawrence's cliff, and both "Amounts" and "Lie" were rip-offs of a forgotten Rites of Spring song), but in hindsight I clearly did have a mild case of sticky fingers.

We decided to release the record ourselves. Colin Sears lived a couple streets over in my Bethesda neighborhood, and was sitting on a Blood Bats record, so he and I decided to start a label called Hellfire—really nothing more than a cool name (courtesy of Ramsey) and a logo. He took cat. #1 and we took cat. #2. I drove the two miles down Wisconsin Avenue to open up a PO box over the line so our label's address would say *Washington, D.C.*

With the photos that Nathan's girlfriend Becky Maury took of us in the alley behind the 9:30 Club (because Bethesda wasn't scary enough), I began laying out our cover; the first of what would be hundreds of covers in my eventual career as a graphic designer. Shawn was into comics and I was into drawing, so we decided to include a Swiz comic book (in what is now known as a "value add"). I printed and assembled the comics and inserts at my old high school graphics art class with my favorite ex-teacher, Mr. Zimmerman.

To make sure Ramsey knew he was appreciated, I put a picture of him also jumping off the cliff, but I didn't halftone it properly so the photo just looks like a black smudge. Shawn always mispronounced Ramsey as "Ramses" . . . it sounded cool and stoic, so I wrote it that way along with a drawing of his dragon tattoo as a special "thank you." I heard later he was kinda bummed by all that, thinking, *Not only did they kick me out, but Jason intentionally ruined my cliff photo, stole my tattoo, and couldn't even bother to spell my name right.*

I mailed the master tape off to Bill Smith Custom Records in California, and in a few short weeks, Shawn, Alex, Nathan and I had our first record (collectively and as individuals) in our hot little hands.

—JASON

THREE SHADES REDDER

I was nervously praying for an anonymous transaction with a random employee when I brought a box of Swiz singles up to Yesterday & Today Records for consignment. Unfortunately, Guy Picciotto was working the register that day.

He grabbed a record from my hand and rapidly flipped it this way and that, laser-eyeing the info, leafing through the comic book, assessing . . . judging. When he slid the 7" out of its sleeve I almost thought he might bite it like a fake gold coin. But, to my horror, he slapped it on the store turntable, dropped the needle, and played it start to finish. It sounded so plinky to me as it flitted through the store. I had to wait through it for the cash or the slip, so I absently flipped through Discharge singles I already owned just to have a place to sink my eyes.

Guy was super cool and supportive, treating the whole thing like a legit transaction, and thankfully didn't seem to notice the last riff was a straight lift from his previous band's reject pile. Even so, I slinked out of there three shades redder than when I came in.

—JASON

MELTDOWN

I had a complete meltdown when Damian for One Word, who opened up and used my drum set, smiled at me after his set and announced he had broken my bass drum head. I freaked out! The show was a really important one for us, opening for Shawn's old band. Luckily the drummer had his drum in the car, and we furiously swapped out the head while the crowd waited. I was so pissed. But he remained calm and said something to the effect of, "Hey, we're just having a lot of fun . . ." I've tried to remember that, because I get too keyed up when I play shows.

—*ALEX*

DAG NASTY

Show flyer, original art
November 11, 1987
Art: Jason Farrell

NOVEMBER 18, 1987

Swiz played the 9:30 Club with Dag Nasty and One Word. It being our second show at the 9:30 Club, we briefly discussed what gimmick could top the smoke machine we had rented for our first show there. All we could come up with was a bubble machine, so we dropped the subject and opted for a straight-ahead approach.

Among the kids in attendance was one rather large and potentially surly elephant in the room. Shawn was the original singer of Dag Nasty, and had written lyrics to many of their classic songs: "Can I Say," "Never Go Back," "One to Two," "Another Wrong," "Thin Line," "Circles," "I've Heard." After their initial shows and a recording session slated to be released as their debut 7" on Dischord, Shawn was unceremoniously booted from the band and replaced by Dave Smalley. The band shelved those gruffer, raw-er Shawn recordings and rerecorded the songs with Dave, which netted the melodic HC album masterpiece *Can I Say.*

That was all two years prior, and Dag Nasty had gone through a ton of changes since (they shed all the members save Brian, moved to LA, broadened their musical style), but some resentment lingered as evidenced by a few lyrical swipes by both camps ("Much" from Swiz, "Safe" from Dag). I loved Dag Nasty, and Brian Baker was certainly a big influence on my own playing . . . but I must admit the possible showdown and potential unfolding of a harDCore soap opera moment left me kinda giddy. Looking now at the original artwork for the flyer, I can see I wrote *From Cali* next to *Dag Nasty*, but walked back that catty swipe with a bit of Wite-Out before Xeroxing. I think this was the last time I drew that "Swiz-man" dude who had become a theme for our flyers (as it was clear that he had simply morphed into a comic book version of Shawn).

We had just gotten 200 copies of our debut 7" rushed out to us a couple days before, and set them on our modest "merch table" of home-screened, water-based-ink T's pulled from an overstuffed grocery bag or whatever . . . (disclaimer: *Please remember to iron before washing*). Ninety-nine percent sure future Swiz bassist Dave Eight helped me set up, as he was our constant companion. Right next to us was the far more impressive plastisol offerings of the Dag merch table. They had recently expanded their items to include sweatpants and their first post-Dischord release: the *Your Mine* single on Giant Records. As a sales pitch to potential shoppers, I pointed out the lower price of our *Down* 7", plus the increased value of having 4 songs PLUS a comic book over 2 songs with NO COMIC BOOK.

The 9:30 Club had so many great things about it, but bad sight lines and a structural pole dead in the middle of the dance floor were not among them. Most everyone I know found out at one point or another what a horrible dance partner that pole could be. There was nothing the owners could do to solve that particular issue (the pole was holding up the rest of the floors above), but they did use that one problem to solve the other by mounting a small crow's nest at the top. Prior to a band's performance, a small employee with a huge video camera would roost in the perch, piping a lo-fi feed of the stage to the many flickering TVs peppered throughout the club. They'd press *record* for a band willing to forgo $50 of their pay for a 3/4" video tape, so we signed on. None of us had a 3/4" player, so I don't recall ever watching it (Alex still has the encyclopedia-sized thing somewhere). But not every band was willing to give up half their pay for posterity . . . It's a shame to think of all the amazing performances briefly caught in CCTV transmission, only to evaporate upon leaving the cathode ray tube.

Glad that tape exists, because I don't remember our set at all.

I totally remember Dag Nasty's set, because at the end Pete Cortner called up Shawn to sing "Never Go Back." Alex, Nathan, and I had no idea this was going to happen, and were surprised to see Shawn saunter up from the back of the club and climb onstage. I've always preferred Shawn's delivery on that song. He wrote it, he lived it, it has always been his over anyone else who sang it. Seeing him sing it then kinda blew my mind, filled up my heart, and put a big goofy smile on my face. This first olive branch did not mend the tensions (more lyrical swipes were to follow), and Shawn admitted he really didn't know how to move or act onstage with his conflicted feelings of having that band behind him . . . but that moment of making nice was a fucking treat to see.

—JASON

YOUR NEW FRIENDS AREN'T NICE PEOPLE

I liked guitar, but when Swiz started up my main focus in life was skateboarding. I'd spend any time out of school skating with my childhood friends Marcus, Chip, and Frido, plus the expanding tribe of East Coast vert skaters centered around a huge metal ramp called Cedar Crest. I had just picked up a sponsorship from Powell Peralta—a spot on their B team (or "flow" team), which meant most of what I got was either seconds or their questionable Boneite decks. But still . . . fuck! It was easy to overlook the little number 2's that were occasionally branded into my free Rat Bones.

Along with the obvious physical demands, skating also had some pretty hefty social ones which required time and commitment. I had to syphon off a little of each to do the band. To be honest, I didn't mind doing this; the level of partying among skaters was getting more fucked up and I was starting to feel a little uncomfortable around the people I'd grown up with. I began to edge outside the circle and compartmentalize things: skating over here, music over there. It felt weird . . . we had all come up together through skating and hardcore at a time when the two felt wrapped up as one; Chip even had an older sister who was active in the scene (Kathy Cashel, later of Norman Mayer Group and Senator Flux). But over the years, my friends had phased out of punk, so their support of Swiz was not without a little shit-giving for my split in focus and delinquency at the ramp.

One Saturday afternoon Chip came out to see us play with Soulside at a Bethesda Community Center matinee. He was tall, funny, and, like the skate scene in which he was immersed, a bit wild at that point. Chip truly had no social pretensions; very much in the mindset of, *If you're cool to me I'm cool to you, and if my friend says you're good, then we're good.* That kind of mentality is why my closest skate friends got along so easily with Shawn and Alex.

When Chip tried to say hi to some of the scene people with whom I'd been spending so much time, he was coldly ignored in this weird, high-school clique kind of way. I fumbled to frame an explanation or excuse for their hard diss, but Chip cut to it quickly and said . . . "Your new friends aren't nice people."

—JASON

PUKE AS WHITE AS COCONUT MILK

One particular weekend we played CBGB in NYC, which in those days would host these (I cringe to think of it now) Sunday "hardcore Superbowl" shows where like 50 bands would play. We were jazzed to be in New York, and I bought a vast amount of coconut Yoo-Hoo (now discontinued), drank like 8 of them, and eventually puked copious puke as white as coconut milk, there upon the Bowery, a boulevard which, throughout its bleak colorful history, has seen many a man vomit or much much worse.

And this was not the last time I would vomit on that particular thoroughfare.

I recall returning from one such show, pulling up to my folks' house in D.C., and literally getting bodychecked by my mom, who had learned of my subpar grades. I had been attempting to conceal my failures from my parents by intercepting the mail. She promptly grounded me, causing us to miss a show we had booked the following weekend, a huge embarrassment.

—*NATHAN*

PISSING IN FRESCA BOTTLES

Harrisburg was on the way to my grampa's house, one in a 5-hour string of towns I'd watched pass by through our VW bus windows on a hundred family trips since before I had memory. It's where Interstate 83 would dump us into a Lemoyne neighborhood to pick up a smaller road, US 11/15, that hugged the Susquehanna River, bisecting the state with Reading and Philly to the east, State College and Pittsburgh to the west.

It also marked the start of a 30-minute ratcheting of excitement as we neared the Red Rabbit in Duncannon—my family's favorite BBQ drive-in whose seasonal schedule held sway over the mood of these trips. When it was closed for winter we sometimes wouldn't stop at all, us kids pissing in Fresca bottles to make good time. That practice stopped the time my dad mistook a used bottle for a fresh one.

From there we'd head up toward Selingsgrove and Sunbury by the Shamokin Dam. Eventually we'd peel off the river to a smaller mountain road through Muncy, Eagles Mere, and Laporte on our way to Dushore.

As Swiz started playing our first out-of-town shows in early 1988, we'd hit some of these same places whose names had always existed for me, though only as mile-markers on a longer trip. To have them expanded to me as a more full existence—to realize each had a scene made up of people kind of like me—was trippy. It built anticipation for experiencing the next town spilling itself like a piñata. That these were my first trips out of state without adults made it even more exciting and revelatory. I'm sure there's a single long German word for that exact collision of feelings.

Our first show in Harrisburg was, for me, our first fun show. No D.C. generational iciness or NYC tough-guy stuff there . . . just pure, young, goofy energy.

—*JASON*

Swiz, CBGB, New York, NY, first out-of-town show
January 17, 1988
Photo: Amanda MacKaye

MY ASS IS HANDED TO ME: PART 2

Subject 1 walked up on you me and Shawn one day (post-skinhead/pre-cop phase, but squarely in our Swiz days). He was a goofy, happy, affable dude . . . it's actually kinda weird he was ever a skinhead. As Shawn and he bantered back and forth, you were becoming increasingly and visibly agitated. Eventually their chat opened to the wider group, starting with intros. He turned his happy puppy face and outstretched hand to you and said, "Hi, Nathan, I'm Subject 1!"

Your face was the opposite—shut, dark, and set.

> "Yeah we've met . . ."
>
> "Oh . . . ? I don't remember."
>
> "You actually jumped me and beat the shit out of me a few years back."
>
> "Huh? Really?"
>
> "Yeah, it was fucked up, and I'm actually not very comfortable standing here right now."
>
> "Aw, man, I'm sorry! I was drinking a lot back then . . . I don't remember meeting you . . ."

Subject 1 looked kind of sheepish, his smile deflated as smaller and quieter apologies fell out, but he puffed up one last time for a semi-jovial goodbye to Shawn and then left us.

Shawn then turned to you and said,
"Why'd you have to bring that shit up?"

—**JASON** *(in conversation with Nathan)*

WHY IS D.C. SO FUCKIN' POLITICAL?

Yeah, yeah, yeah. You know, I mean, I was going down to hang out with Squint and punks that were down in fuckin' Georgetown, but then I'd hang with kids in Bethesda, then hang out with all those Dischord guys or whatever, but I could see how all of it was related.

And I'd hear, "Blah blah blah . . . these people are this way," and, "Those people are that way." I was kind of like, *What?! You're all fucking punk rockers or into hardcore, whatever it is . . . What the fuck? Why is this fucking place so fuckin' political?*

Because I really got into our little world not realizing that other scene . . . they might have had what you call seniority to an extent, but there are long-term extensive wars between the different subsets of that culture.

It was so much finger-pointing; who was the good punk, who was the bad punk, who was healthy for the scene, and who wasn't. And, well, it's a scene—I mean, there's a lot of different things going on—you can't control it. You can have your little piece of it, but you can't put this blanket over it and proclaim it to be "this."

That is some of the whole allure of D.C.—there are other stories. There are other parts of the subculture that were just as creative but simply didn't get that light shown on them . . . for good or for bad, conscious or not conscious.

But I think some people were *very* conscious . . . and even fought to kind of close another thing. "No, no, no, no. *This* is what D.C. hardcore or D.C. punk *really* is."

—*SHAWN*

IT IS WHAT IT IS

It was super bittersweet to hear *Can I Say*.
I was looking forward to being on that record.
I was feeling let down because I had written some of that,
I just wanted to get a thanks . . . I did,
but I was still bummed.

It is what it is though.
I definitely was pissed,
but what else can you do but write lyrics?
So that's where I channeled things.

BIG BEANS

When Shawn first started tracking vocals for the 12" album, he tried to sing for real, like, with melody . . . not yelling. We were perplexed. "Why aren't you yelling?" He got mad and frustrated that we were not supporting him in his attempt to expand his vocal range, so to shut us up he did "Quick," yelling the whole time . . . even when there weren't words.

We all said, "Yeah, like that!"

I think he was bummed.

I never really knew Shawn's lyrics till they got recorded, so I was surprised when he sang "*Lies are not exercises*" over and over at the end of one song, an obvious dig at Dag Nasty. I thought, *Whoa . . . can we do that?* I jokingly said we should use the initials "B.B." as a working title, which ended up on the track sheet and stuck for a while, showing up on set lists long after we changed the name to "Wash" for the album art.

Amanda played the rough mix of the song for her brother Ian that night. He immediately pointed out the blatant Dag/Brian reference (she didn't realize it in the studio). She was friends with Peter Cortner, and didn't feel 100% comfortable putting out our record with that obvious slap. It opened up a long discussion in the studio the next day. No one objected to the spoken reference earlier in the song, it was more the mocking bit at the end. Shawn promptly shut down the debate by saying, "Fuck it, I'll sing something else. Eli, punch me in at the end." Shawn then screamed, "*I'll face you straight to hell!*" It looks so stupid typing those words now, but it scared me a bit when I heard him scream it. We kept it that way.

One night some time later I found myself riding in Amanda's car, sharing the backseat with Peter. He seemed pissed. It was awkward. Can't remember if it was a long ride, but he only said one thing:

"So, what's 'B.B.' about . . . 'Big Beans'?"

—JASON

ALBANY

We played a VFW hall in Albany with Absolution, American Standard, and a few other bands. I think each of us was really turned off by a certain style of hardcore that was coming out of New York City. Not that we didn't like the bands themselves, but there was a "youth crew" vibe that we couldn't relate to.

That said, it was our goal to play extremely loud, aggressive music and to (somehow) be "hard" or tough. Which for me was quite a stretch, in terms of attitude or backing up whatever came out of my mouth.

So we went up to Albany and had a big chip on our shoulder about being hard. Like our music was the loudest. The coolest. The thing with the X factor that everyone's got to get. We were pleasantly surprised by Absolution, because . . . the vibe was similar.

After we played, we headed down to New Jersey with American Standard in the middle of the night. Doing about 90 on the Garden State Parkway, our rear tire blew out when I was driving and the van went into a crazy skid. I tried to correct the skid by counter-steering . . . right toward the Jersey barrier hugging the driver's side of the van as it careened all over the fast lane. The equipment shifted back and forth in the cargo area, and my mind flashed to the several sleeping bodies crammed in the seats behind me.

The van didn't flip. The skidding stopped. We didn't hit the wall, and I limped the car across the highway to the shoulder.

At that point I was reminded of sports. In particular, some wisdom that Coach LaChance, a wrestling coach, imparted whenever we were grappling too close to the wall:

"I know you're tough as nails, champ, but if your head hits that wall, the wall will always win."

—ALEX

PAY ATTENTION

Absolution were tight, heavy, and hard to ignore. But shows can be long and attentions could wane, especially at an American Legion hall with no stage. Bands would have to set up on the ground with the kids, making it hard for anyone in the back to see anything. When they get bored and get to talking, the overall energy in the room would dip.

Maybe Gavin thought he'd stir things up when he suddenly galloped into the crowd midsong, his guitar headstock held out shoulder-high like a rifle or battering ram. The front few rows parted immediately, with the next few scurrying instinctively from the commotion of knees, arms, and feet. Gavin's headstock was eventually stopped by the face of some kid near the back who had been lost in conversation. Gavin turned and galloped back to the band area before the blood hit the floor—his expression unchanged, the song and set uninterrupted.

Later, everyone agreed a broken nose was unfortunate, but the prevailing takeaway at the time was: you need to pay attention.

—JASON

4510

4510 Highland was our Bethesda Dischord house, even if we didn't make the connection at the time. From inception to death, the life of Swiz can be tracked through this house (& a mess of skateboarders & a few other bands). Dick & Carol Farrell still run 4510.

I'd go to 4510 after school, walk right in the door without knocking, directly into the basement, put Jason's SG on and turn up his 1/2 stack loud. He'd be skating. I'd snack upstairs like I lived there, mostly cheese sandwiches. The Farrells are a Miracle Whip family. This is probably one of the only things I disagree with Jason on. We work out song differences/writing/collaboration, but mayo's a problem. Hellmann's is called Best Made in Olympia (where my lady's from). We're Hellmann's. They're Miracle Whip. Yes, I ate a lot of Miracle Whip cheese sandwiches at 4510.

—*DAVE*

MRS. FARRELL

After practice I walked up the stairs from the Farrells' basement and almost bumped into Mrs. Farrell. Exhausted and just home from work, she sat legs crossed and eyes closed on a folding chair with about three inches of ash dangling from the end of her Winston Light cigarette.

I never heard anything but encouragement from the Farrells, who weathered three years of heavy decibels shaking the house. I think Shanda and Allison might have rolled their eyes at us once, but for the most part I think they tried to ignore us, or will us out of their consciousness.

—ALEX

Dave at 4510
Circa 1988
Photo: Sharon Gardner

Chapter 5

ALIVE!

MATCHING VAN KEYS

on toilet-chain necklaces
like dog tags
4 secret generals
pulling at odds
or oddly in concert
affecting velocity and trajectory
fighting in agreement

—JASON

Swiz, Speedway Cafe, Salt Lake City, UT
August 4, 1988
Photo: Trent Nelson

SWASIDE

To keep the band going, Alex and I had enrolled in local colleges while Nathan finished up his senior year of high school. We practiced at least two or three times a week, and spent many of the weekends borrowing my dad's minivan to knock off shows up the East Coast. These short trips were exciting regardless of how good or bad the shows themselves were; we were getting better, traveling with friends, meeting like-minded kids.

With summer coming I was really pushing for us to do a full US tour, but I'd never booked one before. Soulside had already locked their dates with American Standard so I asked Bobby for advice. He was nice enough to share his list of phone numbers with me; said to call these kids and try to string together cities that made sense from a driving perspective (preferably in a different direction from them).

I had no intention of hijacking their tour, but each kid/promoter I called just wanted to put us on their Soulside & American Standard show. With the only string making sense being the one Soulside had already stretched across the US, I asked Bobby what I should do. He said it was cool for us to jump on the tour (god love him) . . . but only till San Francisco . . . and *only* if the money we got paid didn't come out of *their* money.

I confirmed Swiz on the 13-ish easy dates out to SF, then tacked on one more sketchy midcountry show (bookended by thousand-mile drives) to get us back home. That may have been my only real booking contribution. We couldn't take my dad's minivan out for a month, so Nathan traded in his '70s Pinto hatchback for a Chevy van, with his parents generously ponying up the considerable cost difference.

A couple weeks later we all went to Nathan's high school graduation and sat through passionate, long-winded speeches on growth, promise, and inspiration from his A-through-K classmates. Larson, Nathan strolled up to the podium in a blazer and warped tie that paired poorly with his ubiquitous maroon Toughskins. He leaned in close, nearly kissing the mic, and paused before simply saying, "Thanks . . ." The jarring volume jump and overmodulation from proximity effect made the word feel like a sweaty finger jabbing my eardrum. A longer pause followed. He then ambled offstage. It remains one of my favorite speeches.

With that last bit of business set, we were clear to leave. Day one in Connecticut we barely saw the Soulside guys (they double-booked a Pennsylvania matinee which made them super-late for the night show at the Anthrax), so in my mind the tour started in earnest the next night in Boston. After that show, the promoter split the money into two piles for Soulside and American Standard, then pulled 50 bucks straight off the top of Soulside's cash to hand to Swiz.

Soulside was always cool and supportive toward us, even when it was not in their best interest. But I don't recall Scott McCloud saying much after that night (beyond a glowering warning leveled to the whole group: "If anyone tries to flick my balls, I'll punch them in the face!")

By day three the jollier, ball-flicking contingent had affectionately shorthanded the tour name to "SWASIDE." I had all my silkscreen shit with me on tour in case we ran out of shirts to sell, so while stuck in Burlington waiting to cross into Canada, I drew a SWASIDE logo and burned a new screen for a commemorative shirt design. At subsequent shows we'd sometimes set up a janky print operation out of the back of our van and silkscreen it for free onto whatever was thrown down in front of us: one's jacket, the sweaty shirt still on one's back, the hood of one's car, etc. After the tour we threw the screen away and the whole exchange, like the poor-quality textile ink, faded into obscurity.

—*JASON*

SOULSIDE: I WAS ALWAYS PRETTY SURE THOSE GUYS DESPISED US.

Well, there were probably a few things at play. First, Swiz was pretty tightly wound up in its own little group—after just a few months of playing, we saw that things were clicking, and although we were each very different, we formed a tight unit and anything not part of the group existed outside the borders of Swizistan.

If Soulside was anything like us, they had their own thing going on and hanging out with a group of (mostly) younger people playing a music that might not have seemed as "evolved" might have been a bit of a downer.

The fact that we kind of glommed onto their summer tour, kind of hijacking their plans, was also probably a bummer for them.

On top of all that, there were some personal antagonisms that I created all by myself. I had a crush on Scott McCloud, their guitarist. I did all I could to bring some real awkwardness to the situation by doing things like labeling items in his room with sticky notes, and repeatedly calling him from out of state, and calling him my "coast-to-coast buddy," an honorific I still use with him on occasional social media posts. (I also called the Gilman Street warehouse to speak with members of Ignition the evening they performed there just to give them a pep talk about representing the D.C. scene, but that's a different story.)

So, while remembering Swiz fills me with pride and nostalgia, it also brings back loads of humiliation and remorse: for having fits if I didn't play "right" or had equipment problems, for my interactions with others, and most of all, for failing to really realize how talented the people I was surrounded by were until much later.

—ALEX

Bobby Sullivan and Shawn, Wilson Center, Washington, D.C.
Circa 1988
Photo: Sharon Garnder

RENT/JOBS/RESPONSIBILITIES: PART 1 (1988)

. . . those things just made me look at the band like, *I don't know, man . . . I'm a punk rocker*. In my little weird head of philosophy about that, it's just like, you know . . . like surfing. *Fuck it. If I gotta go on the mission, I gotta go on the mission. I'll deal with whatever happens afterwards*, because that was the most important thing right there: doing this music. I mean . . . that's what I was *doing*. That's what I was *really* doing, you know? I wanted to be able to participate, I wanted to tour, I didn't want to miss shows because, well, it's just going to lead to being able to do more of this. This job shit is only fucking temporary, you know?

There were a lot of people that were in that position and had to do whatever they had to do to make their art. Even if they were not conscious of making art . . . I never thought of our music or anything that we were doing as art. I just thought about it as punk rock and roll. *That's what we do . . . and that's what I fucking do. And fuck you, society,* you know?

—*SHAWN*

07.17.88 / NEWPORT MATINEE *(journal excerpt)*

The soundman wanted us to turn down because he had a second show that night featuring James Taylor's son. We refused, so halfway through the first song ("B.B.") the vocals cut out.

At the end of the song, the soundman yelled, "You blew the PA! Show's over!" Shawn yelled back, "I don't believe you!" We tried to run a mic through a guitar amp, but it didn't work . . . finished our set instrumentally, with Shawn yelling acoustically/futilely. If nothing else, it perked the interest of the few people in attendance.

After our set, Shawn cornered the soundman and asked, "Did you accuse me of breaking your PA?" Dude shit his pants and quickly apologized.

Later in the evening I skated an asphalt bank with Matt and some locals while Sebastian Taylor soothed the town of Newport through a perfectly functional sound system.

—*JASON*

ROCHESTER

During the first tour we played in Rochester with Hunger Artist and some band led by a former punk rocker, who was now trying to demonstrate his rock and roll bona fides. I honestly forget who this was—anyway, he earned our complete derision, especially when he cranked into a total nostalgia rocker, "Do You Remember Rock 'n' Roll?" This was enough to get us roaring with laughter. My inhibitions loosened and, egged on by the American Standard guys, I did a stage dive into . . . the floor, where a piece of glitter embedded into my kneecap and festered for the rest of the tour.

—*ALEX*

American Standard van as seen from Swiz van
USA, summer 1988
Photo: Amanda MacKaye

BURLINGTON 1988 *(journal excerpts)*

7.19

Drove all night to get to Burlington this A.M. To kill time we saw an early show of *Coming to America* (dumb). Did nothing waiting till Jake came home . . . skated his ramp for 10 minutes sans pads & with my street deck. As if that wasn't punk enough, it was wet and there was a locked cable across it.

7.20

Went skating again. TIRED. Went to a quarry with a rope swing drop-off: 30-40 feet. No one else in my band would do it . . . weak. Show sucked, we were all tired and it showed. Slept at Jake's again, got drunk, broke the glass of a picture frame.

7.21

Third day in Vermont. Seems like we've been here forever, tour at a total standstill. Note to self: make sure you have a show every day, and make sure none of them is in Burlington . . . lowest point so far. Got the picture glass fixed while we waited for Soulside to finish printing their shirts. Left at dark for the Canadian border.

None of the bands discussed what you say when you try to cross into Canada, we just took up the rear in the 3-van convoy. Watched Soulside pull up to the booth, pause for two minutes, then drive on. American Standard van was next; 2 minutes, then gone . . . (no surprise, Bill can smile his way into anywhere). All this threw me off. I was expecting searches, IDs, something . . . so I was confused and a little sketchy when I pulled up and said, "We're with them!"

The guard lady asked what our stuff was worth ($3,000?), how long we'd be in Canada (6 days?), and would we be paid (Yes!) . . . Apparently that was my fuckup. She got weird and asked about work permits, I said, "You should have them along with the other two bands."

Then she started sketching out cuz Soulside and A.S. were long gone. She made us pull over and looked for an officer to search us, but it was late and no one was around.

I said something like, "Well, half our shows have been promotional. None of us are in charge of this tour . . . maybe the Canada shows are free?" She said we should stick to that story and let us go, happy to be rid of her mistakes.

We caught up with the others at the next rest stop. Nathan started yelling at Bill for abandoning us, Bill was ready and shut him down instantly, he didn't know what was going to happen either (first time I've seen Bill upset). The guys in Soulside all looked puffed up and fat cuz they were each wearing a dozen or so of the tour shirts they'd just printed. They had told the lady they were tourists. I don't think they were actively trying to shake us at the border, but I also felt like they wouldn't be bummed if it had happened.

Turns out our show in Hamilton (a replacement for the original Montreal show that was canceled) just got canceled, giving us a 4-day waste of time till our Toronto show (tho we might get on a Windsor show the night before). Soulside split off to their Toronto show, A.S. and Swiz head to Montreal because what else is there to do? Get there pretty late, drove around looking for a hotel but decide not to spend the $$. So we sleep in the van at the Hilton until a cop car comes. Head downtown trying to find somewhere to park . . . pulled up coincidentally in front of the club we were originally supposed to play. I was worried we'd get in trouble, but later I saw some homeless guy sleeping on a porkchop median across the street, so I figured it was cool & I went to sleep.

—JASON

MONTREAL 07.22.88, 7 A.M. *(journal excerpt)*
I was woken by Shawn laughing. He was pointing at A.S.'s roadie, Floundaman, who was wrapped in a blanket on the median surrounded by morning traffic (the homeless man). I run across the street dodging cars and kick him awake. We all walk around Montreal from 9 to 3, another day wasted.

TORONTO 07.23.88 *(journal excerpt)*
Another day off . . . Another flat and a 5-hour drive to Toronto to see Soulside show at the Silver Dollar. PED are dumb as shit, Soulside were cool, Vandals were somewhat nostalgic. The show was 19+. Everyone is too old here, not just in years but life. All Archie Bunkers in leather. Almost useless to play.

Got drunk at a party and watched Nathan and Bobby flirt with girls using (intentionally?) horrible lines. One girl called them out as cheesy, to which Nathan shot back, "I have a layer of cheese over my entire body that is so thick, if I lift it, it would reveal my soul." It was both disturbing and impressive to hear that just flow out effortlessly like nacho fondue. It laid there for the rest of the night, puddled on the floor, forcing partygoers to walk around it.

In the morning the Swiz van wouldn't move when we put it in gear.
Turned it off and tried again and it worked.
So we left.

—JASON

Windsor satellite
Art: Jason Farrell

WINDSOR 07.24.88 *(journal excerpt)*

Show in Windsor was cool . . . I had the most fun ever, felt like I was floating. We left at 1 a.m. and slept on the roof of the van in a rest stop. Night is more clear out here; saw my first shooting star . . . a quick little slash. Wasted it cuz I couldn't settle on one thing to wish for. As I searched for more, I caught a satellite tracking slowly and methodically across the entire sky. I didn't know you could see them. I wondered if you could wish on that . . . like, would it stick?

—*JASON*

TORONTO #2 07.25.88 *(Swiz, American Standard, Negative Gain at the Silver Dollar; journal excerpt)*

We're in Toronto again, and are now waiting to play.
I'm on the roof.
Thought I had something more to say . . .

(later)
Show was OK, not worth doing again.

SUM UP OF THE PAST (??) DAYS *(journal excerpt)*

Rockford / Rotation Station: A stage in the middle of a skate rink turned into an indoor skate park with street stuff, vert ramp. Skated OK. Nathan wrung his hands like my mom. Ended up skating thru Soulside's entire set (sorry).

Kenosha / the Orpheum: Huge vaudeville theater where Bella Lugosi and the Three Stooges performed . . . stage was too big.

Iowa City was good, people there were stupid, like a deadhead town.

Lawrence, KS / The Outhouse (w / Token Entry, Bullet Lavolta): Played a cinder-block garage in the middle of a cornfield. Out back, we figured out how to play "Where Eagles Dare" right before going onstage. Rad show.

—JASON

Swiz, the Outhouse, Lawrence, KS
July 30, 1988
Photo: Amanda MacKaye

ALL MY LIES ARE TRUE: PART 2

I turned 18 on tour with Swiz. We were in Buffalo, NY, and before arriving I had already had a pretty shitty day.

It was my first time spending my birthday away from my family and I had called home but nobody answered. I spent my last few dollars on the biggest cup of coffee I could get to keep me going through the day. I don't remember where we were the night before but I remember we started the day early for a bunch of punks on tour. We got to the venue and loaded into a second-story show space. It was an unbelievably hot day. We were all exhausted and a little over being all together ALL the time . . . and probably hungry. Anyhow, tensions were high to say the least.

We had been traveling with American Standard. Bill, Jay, Matt and Scott had frivolity to spare—they were firm believers in enjoying life. They disappeared after (during?) load-in and returned with a birthday cake. The drudgery of "get through another show to get home" turned into celebration on the streets of Buffalo.

The show was incredible—the room was packed—it was the hottest show I have ever experienced. There was a haze of steam so thick you'd think people were smoking. The condensation accumulated and finally released as rain in the room. The energy of the crowd surged and the whole place shook with enthusiasm.

I may not have had my parents or my siblings with me on my 18th birthday—but I was definitely with my family. You can't live with someone, or four people for that matter, in 10 feet of rolling living/dining/sleeping/practice space without loving them. And fighting with them. And needing them. And wishing they would leave you alone. Family.

I have a lot of friends who I have known through music and I stay in touch with many of them. But having traveled and worked so closely with Swiz, we are connected in a way that no matter the length of time between conversations or miles between us, it's always like we just rolled out of the van ready to get into the next day.

(End)

—AMANDA

Amanda, Kansas road, summer 1989
Super 8 film stills: Jason Farrell

SAN FRANCISCO 1988

Our van died on the first few feet of the Bay Bridge headed into San Francisco. Turns out this was a brilliant place to break down, as the city tows you for free if you break down on a bridge, just to keep it clear. This was a plus as we were dirt-farmer broke. Handy: they towed us right on up to the front door of the venue, the Silver Dollar I think it was called (or the Covered Wagon?), so we simply dragged our gear out of the non-working van and did the show for no one.

In order to pay for the van repair, I seem to recall us getting jobs. Or at least one of us got a job. I don't know if this is accurate. Regardless, we seemed to be in SF for ages, and I got a tattoo from a friend of Shawn's named Theo (Jax?) who was sort of apprenticing . . . He fucked up a bit and had to gouge out the blotch with something that looked like a linoleum carver, followed up by bleach; that part hurt. I recall listening to *Exile on Main Street* and feeling kind of fat and exposed as I lay there getting tattooed. It was and is a shitty tattoo but that's on me, not Theo.

We then drove straight back to D.C. from San Francisco, direct and with a minimum of stops, propelled by Jolt. Its not like we had anywhere to be, we just wanted to see how fast we could do it.

—*NATHAN*

Dead van
Art: Jason Farrell

COLLECTION: 2
WE JUMPED INTO A VERMONT QUARRY AND FLOATED NEAR ITS CENTER POINT, SUSPENDED ABOVE THE DEEP BLACK PIT.
THEO SHOWED US HOW YOU COULD TAKE ICE BLOCKS FROM THE GROCERY AND USE THEM TO SLIDE DOWN A BAY AREA GOLF COURSE GREEN. ON THE WAY HOME WE SAW RACCOONS IN THE CITY PARK.

A FEW DAYS LATER SHAWN AND JASON RODE THROUGH THE TUNNELS CLINGING TO THE BART TRAIN'S EXTERIOR.
—ALEX (words) / JASON (art)
CRUCIFIX BURRITOS
YES. YEAH, RIGHT, THE ICE BLOCKS . . . AND THE TRAIN THING. BUT DIDN'T WE FUCKIN' MEET SOTHIRA FROM CRUCIFIX THERE? AND HAD BURRITOS WITH HIM IN THE MISSION? I SEEM TO REMEMBER THAT BECAUSE I WAS JUST LIKE . . . "WHAT THE FUCK?! HOLY SHIT!"
—SHAWN (words) / JASON (art)

Swiz, the Dojo, Windsor, Canada
July 24, 1988
Photo: Alexis Fleisig

Socializing at the Wilson Center, Washington, D.C.
Circa winter 1987/1988
Photos: Sharon Gardner

Swiz, Studio 1, Harrisburg, PA
April 16, 1988
Photos: Jack O'Hara

STU

AIR
24 HOURS
AIR-serv

Alex Daniels
Summer 1988
Photo: Alexis Fleisig

Swiz with Ramsey, Positive Force benefit,
Johns Hopkins SAIS, Washington, D.C.
July 25, 1987
Photos: Amanda MacKaye

Jason, Japanese Steak House jump
Circa 1980
Photo: Marcus Wilcoxon

Amanda, Slinkees show
August 24, 1979
Photo: Charlie Rother

Alex
Circa 1973
Photo courtesy of Patuxent Elementary

Dave
Circa 1972
Photo: Steve Stern

Nathan, Washington, D.C.
Circa 1978
Photo: Mom

Chapter 6

SWEET SPOT

RIPPLE AND I

14th Street mini-mart
pig feet a jus, Kools soft pack
Devil Dog, Ripple, and I

—NATHAN

Shawn, Wilson Center, Washington, D.C.
Circa winter 1987/1988
Photo: Sharon Gardner

WHAT DO WE DO WHEN WE GET TO VIRGINIA?

To navigate we used a big map book of the US that was dog-eared, tattered, and smeared with gunk. We got lost a lot. One time, when we were driving in circles, Shawn, who we thought had been sleeping on the bunk above the cargo area, raised his head from his apparent slumber, extended his arm and pointed. "Go that way," he commanded in a stentorian tone.

That became a little bit of a joke. Each of us had them—things we said or did that the others would rib us about. For Dave, it was the time he was behind the wheel on a late-late-night drive to D.C. from NYC. He turned to Jason, and said: "What do we do when we get to Virginia?"

Jason's monotone reply: "Turn around."

That was Jason's thing. The idea that he was a robot, or a cyborg. Is there a difference? With Nathan, it was his penchant for Yoo-Hoos and his tendency to use the tinted exterior windows of the van as a mirror, not knowing (or caring) that his personal hair-care moment was on full display for those inside the vehicle.

Shawn's directions, though delivered authoritatively, turned out to be useless. But another time when we were driving he was an essential copilot. We bombed across the country in about two and a half days, driving from San Francisco to D.C. I was on one of the later shifts, driving through West Virginia on a hilly, windy route full of speeding semitrucks.

I was losing it and Shawn could tell. To keep me engaged, he walked me through the entire comic book universe, introducing me to a pantheon of characters I knew nothing about, and keeping me from nodding off.

Years later, Shawn played the roles of caretaker and ambassador. We were in Japan on what was pretty much a Swiz reunion tour. As Sweetbelly Freakdown, a name that beguiles most, we played several dates in the United States and then played a string of dates in Japan. After almost a decade not playing together, it was a pretty heavy trip to go so far and see so many new things.

I don't, however, think I traveled particularly well. I was hesitant to connect with our hosts, and afraid to make my way through the city. Shawn jumped in headfirst. He seemed to relish being there and meeting people. When I was freaking out about my ripped-up hands, which were torn to shreds because I was out of practice, Shawn calmed me down, and said, "Here's what we're gonna do . . ." He walked me out into the neighborhood in Tokyo where we were playing and navigated the purchase of bandages and some sort of first-aid ointment. All of which came off halfway through the first song. But that didn't matter. What I needed was just a bandmate to tell me that it wasn't just going to be okay; it was going to be a blast.

—ALEX

I GUESS HE READ BOOKS

when nathan brought in lyrics
I didn't understand
where they could have come from

dark and smart
deeper than just
a record collection

—JASON

"JESUS, COME BACK . . ."

nathan lived with grace
down 14th, above a mini-mart
at his window you could smoke and see
the women work the street

they'd take breaks in the store below
off-brand snacks & cigarettes
own the space with their brashness
complain to no one
in particular

—JASON

IT'S A WEIRD THING ABOUT NATHAN . . .

. . . because I always liked the dude, but I just . . . I don't think I was ready for him, you know what I mean? There's so many different weird competing things that were going on with Nathan at the same time. There was his ambitions as a musician himself. Also, just like, you know, the whole fucking hanging-out-with-chicks thing, because, I mean, good god, he was pulling them in . . . and I never understood that.

I was surprised that he had his own, lack of a better word, "artistic air" about him that I think was so far ahead of anything that I was thinking at the time. He just was definitely more well-read and writing things that were like, *Whoa, where the fuck did that come from?* In one way it was super attractive, in another way we wanted to push that down, you know what I mean? But I really liked playing with him because as much as we tried to, like, kind of calm that (artistic air) down, a lot of times he was the one really pushing us to the edge. You know, despite us *wanting* to try something, he was *making* us do it . . . whether that was literally/physically or just through his presence or persistence at having an idea or direction that he wanted to go.

We were really lucky to get him, and have him for a little while . . .
but we totally didn't know what we had when we had it.

—*SHAWN*

TARGET: A.D.

I don't know why, but it stuck. Not only with people in and around the band, but with people who met me decades later. A bunch of people call me Target, or Target A.D., or Targetaldaniels.

It's origin is pretty embarrassing, I suppose. We decided that like rap emcees and DJs, we could come up with some killer nicknames. Mine was the only one that stuck. I picked it because my beat was always "on target."

So yeah. I'm Target.

The other guys' nicknames didn't really last, although there are probably a few people in the world who still call Jason "Cyborg." I don't remember Nathan's or Shawn's names, but later some people called Shawn "Salsa Brown." Not sure if he liked it or not.

Dave Stern. Now there's a guy with some nicknames. Dave Eight. Spidey. And I'm sure those are just scratching the surface.

—ALEX

CYBORG 4510

Jason was so creative, he was so focused and could concentrate. If we needed a T-shirt design a few days before a tour, he could get it done. He'd have us come over, he'd have the inks, the stencil, and we'd knock it out. I'd show up late and do two shirts and he'd have a whole stack done. We'd dry Swiz shirts in the platform of the van, hitting the road smelling of ink.

—SHAWN ✱✦

CONSIGLIERE

Amanda put out our records . . . a de facto manager . . . but also:
friend, gut-checker, 5th member, sister, conscience, staunchest supporter,
consigliere of the Swiz family.
There was no vote.
It just
was.

—JASON

JERSEY COUSINS

Downtime with Bill, Supe, Matt, and J was always loose and goofy, viciously funny. They were to me like cousins from New Jersey, and our tours together felt more like road-trip family vacations. But onstage American Standard was 100% solid 100% of the time. It was inspirational and intimidating.

—JASON

BANDS

Well, American Standard comes to mind, first of all. I think we had a level of kinship and competitiveness that was healthy . . . they pushed us, especially playing live, man. Maybe it's the other way around, maybe we pushed them. But you know what I mean? I think that was a good little working relationship we had with them for sure.

Hunger Artist . . . that band was raw and just real. I liked them because they were really nice guys and they just put themselves out there. I mean, Verbal Assault because, well, they're Verbal Assault. Fucking awesome, man. It was fun playing with them.

Wrecking Crew . . . goddamn. We have to talk about that, because I've such vague memories of that. I remember meeting Elgan and . . . what was the guitar player . . . the redhead guy? Metal-head bassist. Yeah. Yeah. That kid, yeah. They were really fucking cool. And the thing that was awesome about Wrecking Crew is they, like, they kind of believed in Swiz, you know? That's the vibe I really got from them. I was like, "No, *we* believe in *you* guys."

Absolution, of course, because I think just hooking up with them gave us legitimacy in the New York hardcore world. They were really fun and they were cool, and they're an incredible band. Them and I'd say Token Entry, you know, that those two bands—playing with them in New York—is really what got people to start paying attention to us, like, "That band's weird, but OK, they're playing with those guys and they signed off on it and they think those guys are cool . . . we'll give them a little bit of a chance." The Gorilla Biscuits and the Youths of Today . . . we were never going to, like, go along with those guys. We were never going to win. They had their own thing, they had their own package, they have their own fucking crowd. They might've been like, "Yeah, that Swiz band is cool, but . . . we're Gorilla Biscuits," or, "We're Youth of Today." And plus, it just wasn't what we were into.

Every time I looked at anybody in the Icemen, they looked like they just wanted to kick my ass.

—SHAWN

SOULSIDE

SOMETHING ABOUT AMANDA

Amanda's mom used to use the word "gig." I was at Beecher Street one time with Amanda talking to her mom. A Fugazi tour schedule was on the wall. Mrs. MacKaye said, "He's playing a gig in (. . .) tonight." I took the word from Amanda's mom.

Something about Amanda. She knew stuff we didn't. She has a presence. I don't know the show, but she was with us, the show was done, we needed to get paid. Not spoken, but it was obvious none of us wanted to find the courage or hound for the nominal amount. Amanda up and just did it. Made it look easy. It wasn't the sum we expected, it was a bit more—maybe it was 80 instead of 50. But it made me feel stronger.

Amanda made us stronger.

—DAVE

Amanda, Wilson Center, Washington, D.C.
Circa winter 1987/1988
Photo: Sharon Gardner

PUBLIC ENEMY

w/SWIZ

THU MAY 18

Tickets available at 9:30 Club box office, all Ticketron outlets or call Teletron at

THAT TIME WE OPENED FOR PUBLIC ENEMY

Don, Shawn's brother, had
immaculate British Knights
He saw us play . . . once

—NATHAN

Show flyer
May 8 + 9, 1989
Art: Unknown
Courtesy of Frank Hammer

A PUNK BAND FROM D.C.

I'll never forget when Lamont,
my boss at 9:30 Club, walked out
and asked me if we wanted to play
the Public Enemy shows.

I was like,
"Why us?"

And he's like,
"They want a punk band from D.C.
. . . and you're in one."

And I was like,
"OK, no problem."

—SHAWN

DID YOUR FAMILY LIKE YOUR BAND?

Back then? No.
They thought I was a fucking idiot. You know . . .
"What the fuck are you doing, dumbass?
This music isn't going to go anywhere . . .
Why are you yelling?
What are you so mad about?
Get a job at the fucking hospital
so you can have things
like, I don't know,
a retirement."

—SHAWN

MICRO-GENERATIONAL SHIT-TALKING *(a conversation)*

[01:10:02] Speaker 1: "I think it's interesting looking at the division of the scene and the literal plotting and dividing, you know what I mean? Like, 'Hey, G.I. and Black Market Baby are going to get *those* kids. And Embrace—or later on One Last Wish, Fire Party or whatever—you're going to get *these* kids.' Unconsciously knowing that but not really being able to put my finger on what that was . . . I just always saw it as, *Well, OK, these guys have been around, they built this structure. So of course they have the control over things.* You know what I mean? Because they built it.

"But because we were within the structure and allowed to be there and participate, I also felt like we should be able to do it 100 percent unrestricted, whatever it was we were doing. I mean, so maybe some of the actions or things that were said at the time, as a reaction to that, were just the natural jockeying for position and existence.

"I think in any type of art scene or whatever, someone is going to say, 'This painting you're doing is cool, but painting should really be more like *this.*'

"And in a weird way I think, *OK, you say it should be like* that . . . *and* this *thing I'm doing bothers you about my painting? That's cool . . . but now I think I'm going to do* more *of this thing that bothers you.*

"Just being younger and being full of youthful energy dealing with, in some cases, people that were four, six, eight years older than us . . . they had already been through all that. They got all that out. We wanted to express a similar thing. They were just kind of like, 'Hey, man, you know, we've all been there, done that . . . *but* you're still included in this.' And in some cases there's an element of, 'We're going to let you guys be *that* for a while and then hopefully we can mold you into *this*' . . . you know?

"Hanging out with Bobby Sullivan especially, I felt that all the fucking time. I remember some people would say, 'Oh, it's Bobby.' But a lot of cats were definitely in that older crowd . . . they knew him because of Mark. You could just see that with certain people it was, 'Oh, yeah, Mark's little brother . . . and his little friends.'

"I feel like people were looking at us like we were just young hardcore wild-ass jackasses. And because of that, I was like, *OK, I'll be that hardcore wild-ass jackass,* to an extent. In a lot of ways some of the motherfuckers definitely needed to, like, get a little bit of the middle finger to be reminded of who they fucking were. And I mean, you know, it's just like . . . *Punk is fun, motherfuckers. Sorry.*

"People have these perceptions and make these ultimatums in their own head about whatever D.C. music or certain personalities within that are supposed to be. But they're whatever you want them to be, you know what I mean? I think that's exactly what we were trying to do at the time. Not really consciously, but unconsciously doing that. And we also felt like—*I* at least I felt like, I can't speak for everybody, but—I felt like we were also a representation for those younger kids who had that type of energy, wanted to get that out, still wanted to participate and be whatever this thing we call hardcore punk rock was. I felt like in a way we were . . . I don't know if I want to say 'sticking up for' necessarily, but like, you know . . . being the presence for those kids." *[01:13:29][147.6]*

[01:13:30] Speaker 2: "I think a part of that middle-finger thing was just the way that you've got to, like, delude yourself to believe in yourself. Gerrymander your strengths so you feel like you've got the confidence or chops to establish your position or stake your claim. We'd convince

ourselves we got something over another band, which I guess is fine, but then we'd fuckin' say it out loud in an interview . . . 'Yeah, Gorilla Biscuits is popular and all, but . . .' or, 'Sure, Fugazi is great, but . . .' A bad side effect of that distortion, besides a foot in your mouth, is maybe you lose sight of . . . You shut shit out unnecessarily just because of your envy.

"That was the part of the reason we kept rubbing Ian the wrong way . . . We kept jockeying and he's just like, 'You fucking kids talking your shit . . . fuck you! I've been up here doing this shit since you were still crashing your BMX bike. Get the fuck out of here.'" *[01:14:28][58.1]*

[01:14:29] Speaker 1: "Yeah, but you know, we were like, 'Move over, rover.' Any story of musicians of any era has all that shit . . . Look at the fuckin' Rolling Stones and the Yardbirds and all that weird jockeying for position when they were just little kids. It's just natural. There's always a pecking order, the young bucks trying to get control of the pride, you know? Shitty little punk-ass lion with scrap and attitude getting batted down by this grizzled old king . . . just gnashing it out. Circle of life, man." *[01:15:32][33.6]*

[01:15:33] Speaker 2: "See . . . that's kind of what I mean about deluding ourselves . . . like, subtly equating your tiny little band with the Rolling Stones . . ." *[01:15:41][8.9]*

[01:15:42] Speaker 1: ". . . and lions." *[01:15:43][1.9]*

# # #

—***SHAWN*** *(Speaker 1)* / ***JASON*** *(Speaker 2)*

FUN SCENE

I've read some interviews about the "initial ideas" about Swiz, and what sort of aesthetic/sound/mentality we were about that suggest the band was all about reacting to an older "artier" crowd of D.C. musicians. I think there is some truth to this, but I doubt it was a very conscious plan. We were 16-18 years old and we wanted to rock. Plain and simple.

But more important than that, we became quite close. Not just the guys in the band, but a larger group of friends who came to see us play, people we cavorted and commiserated with, crushed on, compared ourselves to, freaked out, trespassed with, and basically gelled with. It was a fun scene. I felt part of it. I felt like I had something to say, or play, and had found like-minded people to do it with.

So stuff about whether we had a certain sound compared to other D.C. bands, whether Jason created a compelling design element for the band (he did!), how we "fit in" compared to other artists, is really secondary to the idea that we were intensely dedicated to something really special. Something we were creating on our own—but at the same time a project that benefited from people who built a scene before us that was nourished by a loving group of contemporaries.

—ALEX

FURY WAS WEIRD

Chris Thomson had some stuff he wanted to express after being in Soulside for a while and we all wanted to do a nasty little pissed-off recording. It was a reaction to where things were—if you thought Swiz was weird, we wanted to see what people thought of Fury. The thing that was cool about Chris—when it came down to it, he was so straightforward he'd be like . . .

"Fuck *this*, fuck *this*,
that's kind of cool,
and fuck *that*."

—*SHAWN* ✱✦

Fury, Safari Club, Washington, D.C.
Circa 1989
Photos: Joe Wongananda

CHRIS THE BAPTIST

I feel like Swiz was in its "sweet spot" over the winter of '88/'89. We were in the rocking chair between our two tours—still tight from the first, not yet jaded from the second. We were playing a ton of local Positive Force benefits, Safari Club and 9:30 Club shows, plus weekend trips all up and down the East Coast. We were happy with our debut 12" that had just come out on Sammich, a label whose two previous bands Soulside and Shudder to Think had been moved up to full Dischord status. We were getting along as well as we ever would and entering our most creative and collaborative writing phase.

Despite these maturations, it was clear that Swiz wasn't going to find a home in the hearts of the older scene. I get it . . . even Dag in '85 was considered a backslide in many eyes, so when we pulled into port a couple years later, the prevailing sense was that ship had sailed and we were just kids cannonballing in its faded wake. (It also didn't help that our mouthier interviews had made their way back home from remote tour outposts.)

Still, it was hard not to take it personally—especially when we were not asked to contribute to Positive Force's *State of the Union* comp, the assorted-chocolates sampler of the 1988 D.C. scene. It felt like being held at arm's length until we fell in line (or in case we didn't). Shawn, Alex, and I kinda said "Fuck it" and hatched a plan to start a project that ran in the opposite direction, one whose sole purpose was to be more hardcore than Swiz.

Fury was the result of surplus: riffs, energy, frustration. I came up with the name and wrote simple, aggressive parts to fit it—ones I didn't feel like debating or adorning through regular Swiz channels. Alex and I would just hash them out quickly. Shawn couldn't really play bass, but I loved that messy bit of chaos. I think he suggested we ask Chris Thomson to be the singer. I don't even know if singing was something Chris had even considered prior to our ask—it just seemed like his energy would be a good fit. (Coincidentally, that was the same way Shawn had ended up a singer via Dag Nasty.) When Chris came over to his first practice down in my parents' basement, he promptly spat on the floor. I didn't really know what to say, so I mentally framed it as a baptism and just avoided that spot as we cranked through the songs, Chris ranting along.

—JASON

SHHH

It's pretty horrible when you
have to look at stuff you actually said
when 16/17/whatever . . .

I just want to hug that kid and say,
"Shhhhh . . . just don't speak, son."

—*NATHAN*

Nathan
Circa 1988
Photo: Rebecca Maury

HELL YES I CHEATED PHOTOS: 1

We all met at Leah Jaffe's house on Wallach Street to take the photos that ended up on *Hell Yes I Cheated*.

Leah had a sweet cat that had eaten rat poison as a kitten. It may not have had a tail. Whether it was the toxins or the lack of a dorsal fin, the little cat could not walk a straight line and its rear would propel forward faster than the front end.

So of course we called the cat Sidewinder.
Leah wasn't impressed.

We dressed in drag for the shoot, which was in the basement. I don't remember the discussions leading up to this, but the gist was that there was a real macho vibe emanating from the hardcore scene, and a very jocky dress code of basketball sneakers and letterman jackets had started to prevail at punk matinees coast to coast. We decided to wear dresses.

Bea Valdes took the photos. I later saw her work at the Corcoran Gallery, which really impressed me. Years later I would occasionally run into her in D.C. and remind her of the pictures, which I think ranked pretty low on her list of creative accomplishments.

—ALEX

Hell Yes I Cheated photo shoot #1
Early 1989
Photos: Beatrice Valdes Paz

"I AM THE BEST DRIVER IN SWIZ"

We were on the highway, maybe near the Maryland House or even in the state of Delaware, when I decided to start a fight with my bandmates.

Well, I didn't actually *want* to start a fight. I just wanted to poke fun at the fact that sometimes things got a little incendiary in the van.

"I am going to start a fight," I announced.
"I am the best driver in Swiz."

"Ha ha ha," my bandmates chortled.
Yes, we were an excitable bunch.
Ha ha ha.

Within three minutes
we almost came to blows.

—*ALEX*

No Punches Pulled CD cover art
Circa 1992
Art: Jason Farrell

BOXER'S FRACTURE

In the van, weeping
is Dave. His hand broke on Shawn's knee,
fingers akimbo.

—NATHAN

100 ON 90 (BOXER'S FRACTURE 2)

A three-show run in January with Soulside and Hunger Artist across upstate New York; maybe Albany, Buffalo, Syracuse? The first night was a DIY affair in a venue that pulled double duty as a community center, with tumbling mats stacked against the wall. A pretty good show—we got paid OK. While we were all standing around, talking with anticipation of the next night (at a proper club opening for 7 Seconds), the promoter found a forgotten wad of moist bills in his pocket . . . maybe 50 bucks. After a few volleys of "You take it!" "No, you take it!" I proposed we lay out a couple mats and throw down Greco-Roman style, Swiz vs. Soulside, winner takes all.

Johnny stepped up and, to be honest, I thought I'd pin him within the first minute. But the motherfucker is wily. We grappled and squirmed ourselves into a stalemate, broke apart, and reset. I saw an opening and went for a grab. He must've read it cuz he moved a bit as I was going in so I ended up slamming my hand into his hip. It didn't hurt, but it definitely didn't feel right. With my good hand I tapped in our roadie, Paul Dever. Johnny tapped in Soulside's far-larger roadie and we watched poor Paul get thrown around while I assessed my lumpy fist.

I left the emergency room with a right-hand cast that made holding a pick near impossible, and muting out of the question. I was a one-trick pony in that way, so we had to cancel the remaining run. With nowhere else to go, we tagged along the rest of 90 West out to Buffalo. The next night my feelings swung between pissed and psyched as I watched 7 Seconds and Soulside just kill it in what would have been an amazing show for us to play.

We had a bunch of unspent energy after the show, so we drove to Niagara Falls. Being the middle of the night and dead of winter, there was no one there to stop me from hopping the barrier and running out to a rock ledge overhanging the falls. The sheer drop coupled with the sound and power of all that water moving down was mesmerizing—I could feel its mass and volume create a gravity that became stronger the longer I watched. I felt lighter, smaller.

Alex broke the spell with repeated yells for me to get the fuck away from the edge. I teased him about being such a mom or whatever, but I was fully drained of the bravado that had brought me there, and relieved to back away under the cover of appeasing Alex.

I don't remember who ended up with the 50 bucks.

—*JASON*

DOWNSHIFTING

I drove the Swiz van down to D.C. from Boston where I was visiting my girlfriend. For some reason, the headlights stopped working. In the middle of the night. Good thing the bright lights were still functioning. Problem was, the light handle wouldn't click into place. I had to drive about 400 miles holding the light bar toward my body with my left hand, which became severely cramped by the time I crossed the Rhode Island border.

To stay focused, and as a way of ignoring the hundreds of cars going the other direction on I-95 I was pissing off, I wrote a song in my head. It was "Roadtrip," a song about our trip to Buffalo, Rochester, and Niagara Falls. On the way back from *that* trip, Jason performed an even more difficult drive. We were crammed into the back of his stick-shift Toyota Supra, which had questionable bodywork and not nearly enough space for the band. (Where was the van?)

Jason had broken his right hand wrestling with Soulside on the trip, forcing us to miss opening for 7 Seconds in Buffalo. He drove all the way home with a pack of foul, cramped guys, and used his left hand to shift gears. He may have even had to roll-start. Did he have to roll-start?

—*ALEX*

DEAD BOYS

I remember two things about the Dead Boys show we played at the 9:30 Club:

1. Andy Rapoport was there, to show his love for the Dead Boys, rather than go to the huge D.C. local show three blocks away at d.c. space, and

2. Cheetah Crome rolling in the load-in entrance and yelling out to the room, "Where's tha pissah?"

—*ALEX*

THINGS I'M SURPRISED I FORGOT:

Having opened for the Dead Boys at the 9:30 Club: Probably because we were barely there. In fact, barely anyone was there. We left after our set and rushed across town to catch the tail end of the Soulside/Verbal Assault/Fugazi show at the Wilson Center. It was sold out, so we all broke in through a side window just as Soulside got onstage. (Sorry, Mark!)

Having played a show with (almost) all future Swiz members: In early 1986 Carpe Diem (Alex), NFC (Nathan), and Bells of.. (me) all played a Bethesda Community Center show with Gray Matter and Dag Nasty—might've been Dag's first D.C. show after having just kicked Shawn out. Were it not for a flyer and Sohrab's video evidence, I would have denied having played. But I *do* remember attending, and have a vivid memory from Dag Nasty's set: the eddy of slam-dancers mildly disrupted by Shawn. He was anchored at the front with his arms braced against the stage. His eyes were closed, head lowered, and jaw clenched as his ex-bandmates bopped about in their new all-blond look—Dave Smalley singing Shawn's words over his own head.

Having played the Wilson Center: Which is weird because I had seen so many shows there over the years and would have considered it a rare honor.

—*JASON*

Show flyer, Wilson Center, Washington, D.C.
March 24, 1989
Art: Unknown
Courtesy of Positive Force

Fugazi
Swiz
Holy Rollers
Edsel
8 PM $5
March 24th
Wilson Center
positive
force d.c.
Benefit For The
Washington Peace Center
276-9768
heat resistant
Mark

Swiz at the Wilson Center, Washington, D.C.
March 24, 1989
Photo: Alexis Fleisig

Chapter 7

ALIVE II

(Dead by Dawn)

NO BUY-OUT

No buy-out, no time
to eat grocery store hoagie
'neath driver's seat: change

—NATHAN

Swiz second US tour
Summer 1989
Photos + Super 8 movie stills: Swiz

Swiz, the Word, Salt Lake City, UT
August 8, 1989
Photo: Unknown

Jason and Mark Abshire, Post Falls, ID
August 7, 1989
Photo: Alex Daniels

VERY
TYPICAL
NATE
PIC

Nathan and Amanda, San Francisco, CA
Summer 1989
Photo: Unknown
Handwriting on back: Unknown

BADLANDS

—**ALEX** *(words)* / **JASON** *(art)*

WE TOLD GHOST STORIES IN THE DARK VAN AS LIGHTNING BOLTS SHOT ACROSS THE SKY OVER THE BADLANDS IN THE DISTANCE.

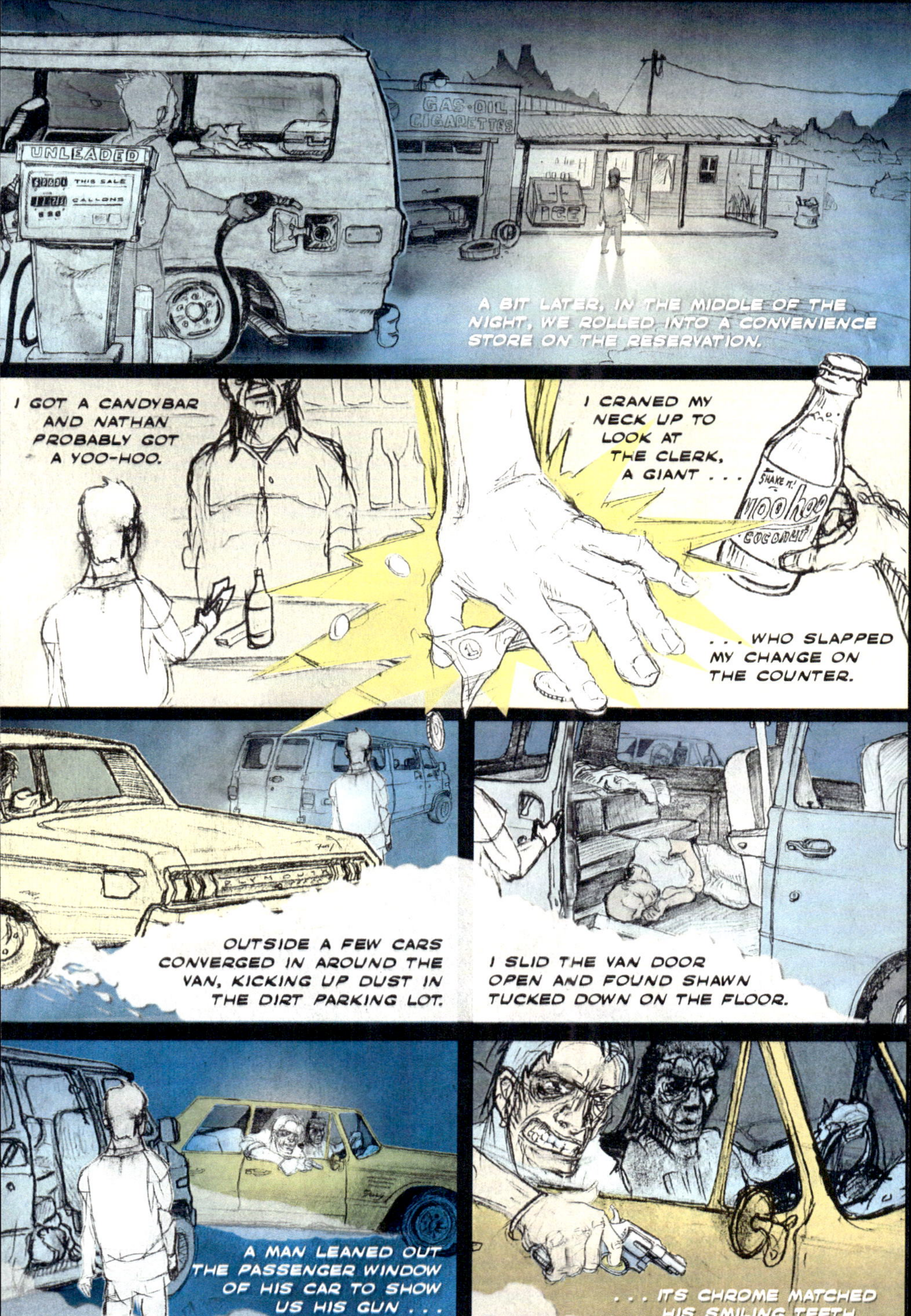
UNLEADED
THIS SALE
GALLONS
GAS-OIL
CIGARETTES
ICE
A BIT LATER, IN THE MIDDLE OF THE NIGHT, WE ROLLED INTO A CONVENIENCE STORE ON THE RESERVATION.
I GOT A CANDYBAR AND NATHAN PROBABLY GOT A YOO-HOO.
I CRANED MY NECK UP TO LOOK AT THE CLERK, A GIANT . . .
SHAKE IT!
YOO-HOO
COCONUT
. . . WHO SLAPPED MY CHANGE ON THE COUNTER.
OUTSIDE A FEW CARS CONVERGED IN AROUND THE VAN, KICKING UP DUST IN THE DIRT PARKING LOT.
I SLID THE VAN DOOR OPEN AND FOUND SHAWN TUCKED DOWN ON THE FLOOR.
A MAN LEANED OUT THE PASSENGER WINDOW OF HIS CAR TO SHOW US HIS GUN . . .
. . . ITS CHROME MATCHED HIS SMILING TEETH.

Photo: Alexis Fleisig

BEN IS DEAD
INFEST
Pearl
EXIT

924 Gilman Street, Berkeley, CA
July 29, 1989
Color photos: José Parral
B+W photos: Josh Stanton

DATE	SHOW	PAY	MERCH	TOTAL
7/7	THE PIT ATLANTA GA.	100.	111.	$211.
7/11	WHST HATTIESBURG MIS.	43.	6.	49.
7/13	AXIOM HOUSTON TEX.	70.	0.	70.
7/4	AXIS FT. WORTH TEX.	250.	~~300.~~ 350.	600.
7/16	LIBERTY LUNCH	27.50	91.0	118.50
7/17	STUDIO G MEMPH. TEN.	138.	40	178.00
7/20	CHURCH IOWA CITY	70.	31.00	101.00
7/21	OUTHOUSE LAWRENCE, KS	156.50	~~156~~ 152	~~312.50~~ 308.50
7/22	GRANDPA'S RIBS LINCOLN NEB.	80.0	62	142.00
7/23	UC BOULDER	100	?	1?.
7/24	ROKIN TP. SANTA FE	30	53	83.00
7/28	LA / PONDERS	50	0	
7/29	BORK	275	8	
7/31	LA / COUNTRY CLUB	85		
8/3	SAN FRAN / COVERED WAGON	140	26	
~~8/5~~				
8/5	SEATLE	157	133	290
	SPOKANE	61	?	
		54	48	

10% OF NOTHING

The first leg of our second US tour had us headed through the South with Shudder to Think. It started with a 14-hour drive from D.C. to Atlanta. As for the show #1, I only remember a chain-link fence and bricks . . . I'm guessing that was the parking lot. What followed was the sudden cancelation of all our Florida shows due to a rash of skinhead violence.

With the Sunshine State off the schedule and days to kill, we meandered toward our newly christened show #2 (née #4) to be held in a double-wide trailer in Hattiesburg, Mississippi. We spent some of our downtime wandering the town's tiny zoo where a grizzly bear paced relentlessly in his small rusted cage while his neighbor, a slack-jawed lion, lolled in a drugged stupor. We stared at them until we couldn't anymore.

It was around this time we started to lose faith in our booking agent, Johnny Stiff. Months after it was all over, he called to get his 10% cut of the earnings. I asked him, "What's 10% of nothing?"

—JASON

Left:
Swiz tour ledger
Summer 1989
Handwriting: Multiple

Above:
Swiz 1989 summer tour flyer
Art: Jason Farrell
Courtesy of Andy Coronado

6TH OF JULY *(journal excerpt)*

We split at 11:15 going south toward Atlanta, hungry & hot being two words that spring to mind. Once again this touring marks a point in my fucking life in which I will have nothing to return to or for—home, job, etc. But in all honesty it's my choices bad or good which left me thus, so the point is moot. I guess I secretly love the hell out of this amorphous living. It keeps me on my toes . . . Hey, this shit had better be top-notch cause I can name more than one place or face I'd rather fucking be.

7TH OF JULY *(journal excerpt)*

Atlanta, GA—show full of sweat, hotter than anything ever, my arms were like rivers. Broke a string in the third song & had to use an alien bass which succeeded in throwing me off for the whole set. Felt like shit, wanted to go home and cry.

8TH OF JULY *(journal excerpt)*

Still Georgia on my mind & body, our two shows in Florida have been canceled. We have a few nothing days until the next show in Mississippi, and god knows they will be nothing days.

—NATHAN

THE SOUTH WAS WEIRD

. . . but some of it I wasn't really sure was about racism. I was a black punk rock kid with other punk rock kids, so was I being treated differently because I was a black kid or a punk rock kid? If something is happening like that, I would think that people are being fucked up to me because I'm a punk, or because I have tattoos, or someone doesn't like my hair . . . I didn't think there was some racial slant right away. I don't remember too much blatant racism back then; I really overlooked a lot because there was so much anticipation about touring and seeing new places that we tended to overlook the little bumps along the way.

—*SHAWN*

UNRELATED QUOTES *(recorded on the back of the tour ledger, 1989)*

Nathan: "The South smells like shit."

Alex to Nathan: "Is that right, dammy?"

Texas man to van: "Y'all near the stockyard!
Y'all need to get the hell outta there!"

FRESH STRINGS

I hated playing a show on fresh strings—they'd quickly fall out of tune as the metal would settle in. So I'd pre-stretch the fuck out of them all up and down the neck till they had no give nowhere . . . then stretch them again for good measure. It kept them true, but left them weak. So I broke strings . . . a lot. My bridge would just eat them.

Years before, my friend Lawrence had shown me a budget way to fix a broken string by rewinding the long end around the tiny ring at the nubby end (assuming you could find it). For it to work, you'd have to leave the excess string lengths dangling from the tuning pegs—to this day I still don't cut string tops. In this way I could squeeze another show or two out of them (or finish the show I was playing if I could fix it fast enough). Show sweat would eventually make the strings totally dead, meaning I was back to stretching the fuck out of a new set.

While restringing my SG before some show, I looped the dead ones together and threw them back in the case rather than in the trash. A couple nights later I wrapped the next set of dead stings to the first, absent-mindedly starting a ritual that stretched a year or more across two tours, snowballing into this rusty halo from almost every show.

It hung out in the guitar case for a few more years . . . then spent the next 30 popping in and out of various storage boxes, comingling with other nicknacks of mishmashed eras, re-earning its continued existence with each passing decade by simply continuing to exist. Now I just keep it because I've had it far longer than I haven't.

—JASON

Show strings collected between
July 1988–August 1989
Photo: Jason Farrell

16TH OF JULY OR THEREABOUTS *(journal excerpt)*

I don't fucking feel like writing Texas this morning waking up and dragging across the floor of this foreign house. Crawling outside, the sun kicked me in the dick like I was a cave fish or some vampire or something.

My hand can't hold the pen hardly, my body is so weak + tenuous today it's like skin over so much water. I just tried to speak & I sounded like a dusty croaker. I need something to drink.

I suppose I should talk about shows—night before last here in Fort Worth was incredible with many kids shaking & swimming & diving & going out of their minds. Did a video interview post-show. Its was a big booster considering the night before we played Houston to literally no one for zero bucks at this huge fucking club. We threatened the promoter until he slid us cash. Got a cheap motel, school-room style TV set playing Westerns and bad news . . . appropriately, you know.

17TH OF JULY TODAY *(journal excerpt)*

Show last night in Austin; small, stupid, nothing to report. I thought Atlanta was hot, I hadn't seen nothing. The sweat is a permanent aspect of my wardrobe, like underwear, body armor, it's very fucking hot & there's not a damn thing to be done about it . . .

Last night we made a tired stop at a Hardees off the freeway & I watched some guy get increasingly pissed as his girlfriend flounced & flirted with some neighboring construction types. Finally this guy gets up and storms out, leaving his girlfriend for a cheesecake, she bubbling & giggling & spouting innuendos, suggestions & racial jokes. As we were leaving, he came ripping through the parking lot & yelled, "Tell that bitch inside what I did to her car!" before speeding away. We never saw her car but I don't doubt his seriousness. Very cute, men & women, women & men . . . we pass all the ugly Southern people & I wave & smile at everyone because I'm a fucking friendly fellow.

—NATHAN

SAM McPHEETERS

We nearly called our second album *Sam McPheeters*. Didn't know him, never met him, but he had given our first album a funny, enthusiastic review in his zine, *Dear Jesus*, and we needed to call the new record something. In my mind it remained a front-runner till a late-morning breakfast in some Southern diner.

Flipping through the booth's jukebox of unheard, third-tier country songs—reading the titles out loud in that annoying way—one title stopped us dead . . . too good not to steal. It was quickly set down in a unanimous vote, and through lips glazed with egg yolk and toast bits, we spat out cover concepts to match the name *Hell Yes I Cheated*.

—JASON

CALLIGRAPHY LOGO

That was part of the concept for our second album, *Hell Yes I Cheated*. We thought a fancy, high-society-invitation vibe contrasted against our rough music would be, I dunno . . . something. So the logo had to be regal. I drew a sketch of it about an inch across . . . we liked it. I spent way too long trying to redraw it at 12" for the cover, never really getting the same feel as the sketch. Alex said, "Why don't you just enlarge the first one on the Xerox machine?" Duh . . . it worked great, and added a roughness that I couldn't get from drawing it large.

—JASON

Swiz, Studio G, Little Rock, AR
July 18, 1989
Photo: Amanda MacKaye

JULY THE 18TH *(journal excerpt)*

Good show in Memphis last night in spite of the absence of a sound system. Memphis is the "home of the blues" but all I saw was a Federal Express convention & their polyester pantsuits & bbq'ed chicken.

On the road to St. Louis, pretty skies, loud music. Jason is brushing his teeth & spitting out the window onto the surrounding cars. I bought some cheap, horrible, vomitus cigarettes and they're worthless. Shawn sleeps for a switch.

All is well. 8:15 pm.

—NATHAN

Swiz van dashboard
Summer 1989
Photo: Amanda MacKaye

SWIZ

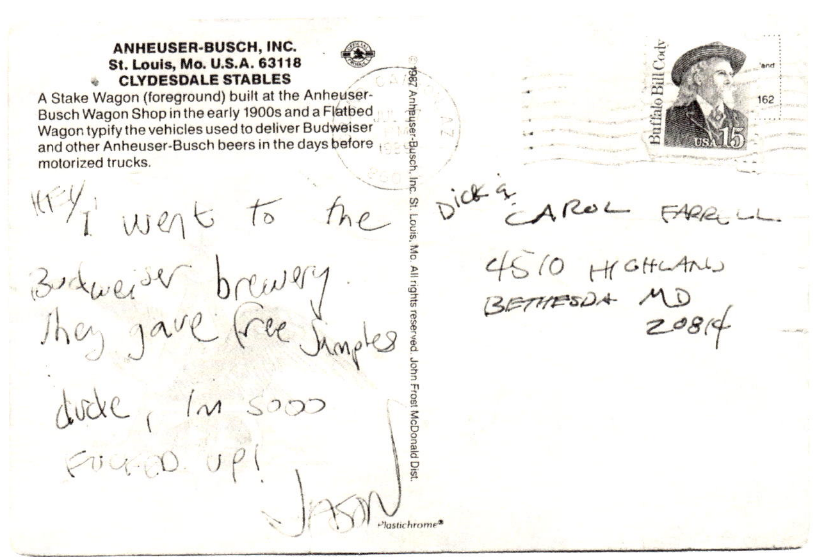

ANHEUSER-BUSCH, INC.
St. Louis, Mo. U.S.A. 63118
CLYDESDALE STABLES
A Stake Wagon (foreground) built at the Anheuser-Busch Wagon Shop in the early 1900s and a Flatbed Wagon typify the vehicles used to deliver Budweiser and other Anheuser-Busch beers in the days before motorized trucks.

© 1987 Anheuser-Busch, Inc. St. Louis, Mo. All rights reserved. John Frost McDonald Dist.

Plastichrome®

Buffalo Bill Cody USA 15

Hey! I went to the Budweiser brewery. They gave free samples dude, I'm sooo fucked up!

Jason

Dick & Carol Farrell
4510 Highland
Bethesda MD
20814

Tour postcard
Summer 1989
Courtesy of Dick and Carol Farrell

20TH OF JULY *(journal excerpt)*

Spent a day in St. Louis yesterday & checked out the Busch brewery. Drunk on beer and King Cobra Malt Liquor samples at 2 p.m., sick at 7 or 8. Iowa City today, show in a church. We'll see . . .

22ND OF JULY *(journal excerpt)*

We were supposed to have a day off, but this morning I get shaken awake & told we're playing in Lincoln tonight. Fell asleep in the shower & I never wanted to leave and now at 3:55 we're on the road again. Blah blah blah blah fucking blah. Amanda and I had a little tiff last night & I could not care less. Just part of the territory—corn, wheat, grass, browns, greens & multicolored cows, I just don't give a shit.

(Later . . .) Another show to all of 20 people, no sound system, period.

—*NATHAN*

DRY LIGHTNING

I don't think I believe in ghosts
but on a black night driving fast
through the dakota badlands
the sky and land were alive
moving with and against each other

where they rubbed, old electricity warmed up
static bits of a thousand years
gathered and rolled into dry lightning
that flash-lit the hills, hunched and creeping
closer in each dark intermission

leaned in, eyes at the windshield
van like a faraday cage
speeding through the heart of the union
becoming charged particles
anxious, exhilarated, on
being made aware of elements, gravity
eons and always

it was a language I don't know
but the message was clear
we are here

—JASON

JOHN C. FLOOD, INC.
PLUMBING · HEATING
AIR CONDITIONING

INTERMITTENT SOLENOID

The van would only start in the mornings. I don't know why, it seemed fine in every other way, but shutting it off once warmed up was risking a very long vehicle nap. Strategies and superstitious rituals were quickly developed and scorn was heavily dropped on whoever fucked up and forgot them.

To avoid being stranded we'd have to leave the van running all day. We'd lock the doors while it idled if we needed to step away, e.g., pee, eat, or visit the Grand Canyon. At first I was worried it would get stolen, catch fire, or just die in the summer heat while we were gone. But it was always there, still running, ready to go.

At night I'd hope we were putting it to bed early enough for a full night of cool mechanical sleep. Some mornings it woke easily, others it felt like sleeping in a bit longer.

A gas station guy said we needed to shut our van off to fill up. We told him why we couldn't. He popped the hood and took a look, figured out it was something we couldn't afford. So he showed us a trick: strip the purple wire coming off the fire wall and jump it straight to the battery post with a coat hanger. Not really a "hotwire" kinda thing (you still needed the key), but it worked every time.

The underlying issue could have easily been fixed with 200 bucks and a half day's wait, neither of which seemed affordable. So instead this extra step was just adopted into the growing list of weird tasks that made up standard operating procedures. And for the next month or year or whatever (long after the tour was done), that's how we'd start the van: a two-person job with one behind the wheel, the other under the hood. It was kind of fun, more fun than regular starting.

When I was sitting behind the wheel, I'd watch through the glass as whoever had coat-hanger duty would do their part. If I could resist honking the horn, I would see in their face an air of purpose, a glimmer of pride, like, *Yeah . . . we know the purple-wire trick.*

—JASON

Swiz, Grand Canyon
Summer 1989
Photo: Amanda MacKaye

TONIGHT! HOLLYWOOD!

It turns out it's far
to the Whisky a Go Go
on a borrowed bike

—NATHAN

NASTY, BUT SOMEHOW SUCCESSFUL

I was living in LA, downtown in a one-room flat with Mark Abshire. We were bike messengers. We were broke. We had a jar of peanut butter we shared nightly for dinner when we moved up from Orange County. Lunches were bought with an another old jar filled with change. We split it equally based on the day's countdown till the next paycheck. 55 cents a day. In 1988 you could go downtown, to Grand Central Market, get week-old Entenmann's just on the verge of mold, but not! It was nasty but somehow successful. Mark paid for Denny's Grand Slams after our first check.

Swiz came to LA and thankfully pulled Mark and I outta there onto tour. I think we had to sneak Amanda into the flat to sleep cause the two families we shared a kitchen & bathroom with were appalled there was a girl traveling in a van with all these guys.

—DAVE

GILMAN STREET

We had always talked ourselves up a good deal, about how we would melt the stage and that a perfect end to a set would involve the total collapse of the venue—a complete, chaotic meltdown of amplifiers, strings, guitars and drumheads. Comic book stuff.

At Gilman Street we decided to put on suits and put our total fantasy show into action. I don't know if it was my idea, but somehow I got the nerve to conclude our set by running through my drum set into the crowd a few bars before the end of our last song. I don't know what the effect was, but I think I got my sneakers ensnared in some cords and it felt a bit awkward.

The soundman came up onstage before the next band and tossed my drums on the floor, showing them the same disregard I had just shown for his gear. Totally humiliating.

—ALEX

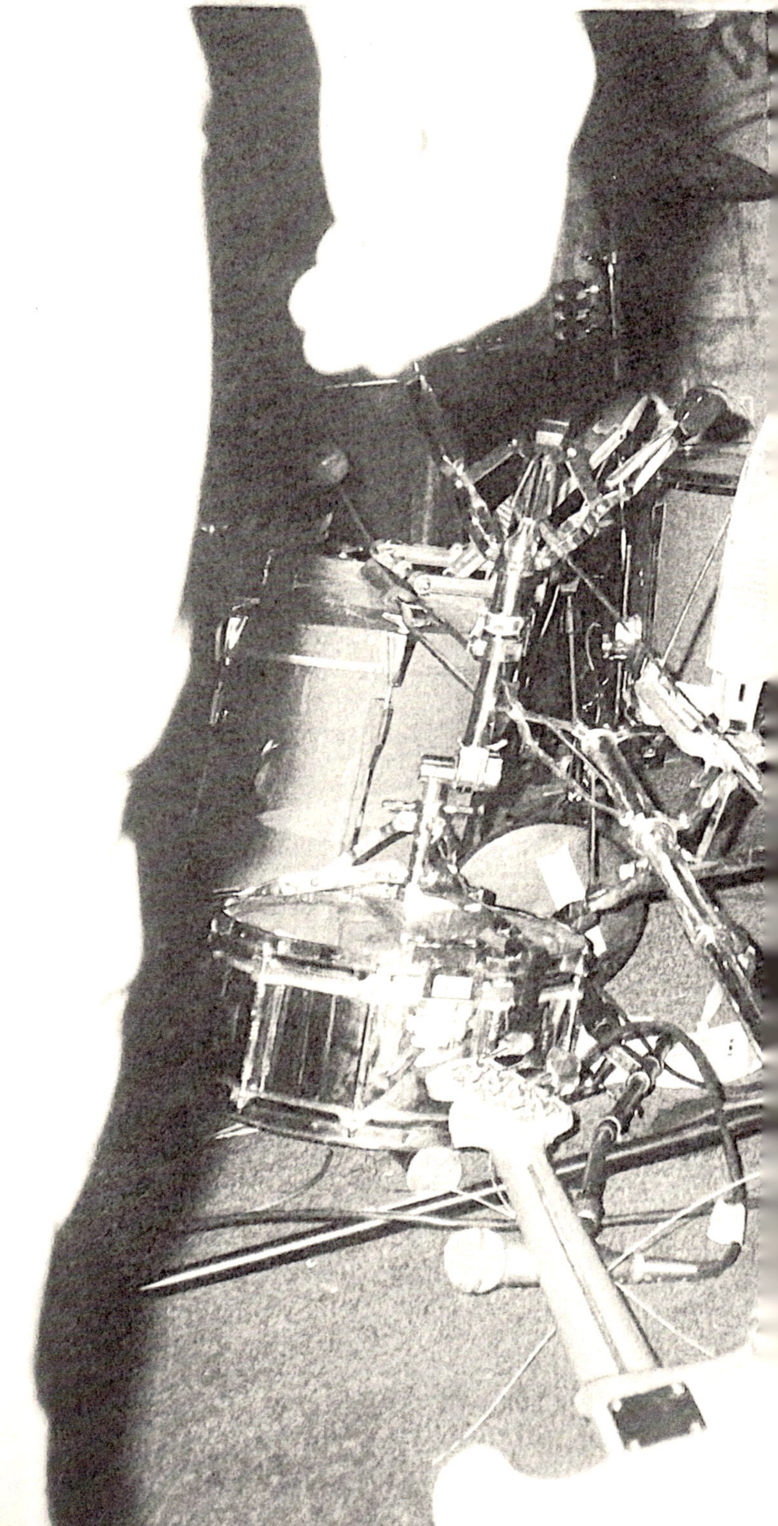

Swiz, Gilman Street, Berkeley, CA
July 29, 1989
Photo: Josh Stanton

SAN FRANCISCO, 3 OF AUG *(journal excerpt)*

Shows like this:

Fenders, LA: Nobody there, huge place, no money, shitty in general.

Gilman St, SF: Good show, great turnout, wore suits. . . still dissatisfied, can you dig?

Country Club, LA: Huge place, good turnout; assholes, no money, private dressing rooms, bullshit.

Back in SF at Covered Wagon—weak & I got onstage drunk as shit which shouldn't be done . . . Many punk rock stars present & girls oozing here and there to flirt with & get pissed off about, so it was a busy night, you know . . .

Lord, set me free from this nonsense, please please please! I hate the music & I drink too much . . . Hey, like the other night we get to LA, I wound up at Venice Beach in the ocean with my suit on like a big brown flounder . . . & in SF last week I slept on the floor of a tiny room while people fucked violently all around me. California is fast.

—NATHAN

CRUELTY/CAMARADERIE

I could tell he was going through a really difficult time because he had become fucking unbearable. We helped him cope the only way then known: give him shit till he snapped out of it . . . which he didn't.

Now hate myself then for having fallen in line so eagerly with that unsaid hierarchy: youth dynamics when there's blood in the kiddie pool.

Still, I felt fiercely protective. His being 1-of-4 beat out our 3-on-1; a closed-circuit tight unit whose internal dysfunction betrayed no external expression. No one outside could take a swipe.

—JASON

A BITTERNESS BORN OF ENVY

watch them sign their
"X" on the line to ride
a circle of coattails
straight-up sucking
all the air
out of america

while we cut
socialist rations
lunch meat on starches
snickers and cokes
old baloney floats
loose in the van
in thawed water
in the cooler between
shotgun and driver

can't afford "and"
just "or"
gas or transmission fluid
coffee or cigarettes
miles or sleep

the distress was in all ways
artificial
money could be wired
and safe beds existed that would
cushion any fall if the bottom fell out

but that would demand
a tail-tucking admission
of failure

—JASON

AUG 5, 1989 *(journal excerpt)*

Best things about Cali this time around:

1. Got *Queen's Greatest Hits*
2. Jello Biafra told me "the first tour is always the worst" & this is our second terrible tour
3. I had a (2) good meal
4. Cig. have a 50¢ tax so a pack is $2

I would never live here, on that you may quote me.
En route to my old stomping grounds in Seattle
which will certainly be strange.
Memory is a funny thing &
none too accurate, I suspect,
we'll see . . .

—NATHAN

POST FALLS: ELEGANT AND OTHERWORLDLY

The art gallery owner with the wispy beard (Lance? Dale?) made us the kind of pancakes I wouldn't have been able to appreciate for another decade: artisanal . . . packed with nuts and soft cheeses, maybe morels and sprouts? Maybe not, somehow I remember it more like an omelet. But my memory is fickle. For example, many years later when he and I crossed paths digitally, I relearned his name was actually Dave something and that his beard was, he assured me, never wispy.

Having recently picked up *our* Dave (Eight) and his roommate Mark Abshire in LA, our two-band posse (Swiz and American Standard plus Amanda) had swelled its ranks to 11. We had stayed the night at a house rented by three girls who were at the gallery show. They were very cool for letting us spill across their floor. I wish I could say we mirrored their kindness with reciprocal etiquette, but given our age, the era, and acquired inertia from previous acts of semi-shitty behavior, I doubt we did. Recently, Amanda reminded me that they stole Dave's shoes for some reason, so I guess I shouldn't feel too bad.

Yet another hole in the tour schedule meant a second night in Spokane, leaving the day free. The three girls took us across the state line, just inside Idaho, and pulled us off on the highway shoulder. A short walk ended at the top of a deep gorge where the Spokane River and a day of swimming swirled lazily below.

One of girls—Allison—showed me and Mark where to jump: middle of the trestle to the middle of the river. We filled the gorge with loud sounds, hoots and/or hollers, as our arms swung and legs kicked all the way down till high-tops slapped the water, big as mortars.

Allison stood on the railing once the echoes died out and crossed her arms like a nesting vampire. With a small hop she shot the 50 feet straight and silent as a dart . . . no splash as she slipped through the water below.

—JASON

COLLECTION: 3

We were eaten by ants
at an Atlanta swimming hole
and jumped off the rocks
in Post Falls, Idaho.

We crashed a place
in Kansas City for a few days
as the tour meandered, and kind of
wore out our welcome.

We did that in Spokane, too,

and most definitely in San Francisco.

There was some guy (the promoter?)
we stayed with in Seattle whom
we called "Cheeto-head"
behind his back.

—ALEX

GET IN THE VAN

Its definition is maybe the most true sense of "Hate/Love." Sometimes the first memories of touring that pop up are stranded moments.

Bluetip—El Paso in the dead of summer, Wisconsin in winter.
Red Hare—simply stuck in our hometowns.
Swiz—Boulder in hot summer.

Touring is kinda like a constant state of damage management. Shows are canceled, we haven't left our previous city yet, we stay/park close to working pay phones to check in with the next happening gig. 5 dollars a day was a standard daily budget for each punk in the van. Seems like a number lodged in our heads from the price of shows.

On $5 a day we didn't know how to eat. You receive your 5 in the morning and you need to survive all day. There isn't a money machine around the corner. They don't exist yet. No technology actually exists yet to dig you out of this 2,000-mile-from-home hole. The only way to get money from Washington, D.C., is to have it wired.

You have nothing to do in this town. You have nowhere to go. Except for the 30 kids that came to the show last night, you don't know anyone here. Those 30 kids have a life to go back to the next day. They don't realize you're stuck in front of a burrito shop in a hippie town with no plan. The van is the center of your world.

The other van band you're touring with has somehow disappeared. They've found a way out. They know someone/somewhere to go. Their situational recovery plan is one step better than yours. They've done more van tours. I get my 5 dollars. Shawn gets 5 dollars. Nathan gets 5 dollars. Alex gets 5 dollars. Amanda gets 5 dollars. I do not play the bass in Swiz during this tour episode. I am the friend/roadie/whatever dude/space-taker-upper while stuck in Boulder. Be aware there is absolutely no sensible way to spend 5 dollars over a 24hr. period.

The van has a portable cooler. It doesn't have ice. I got a steak & cheese. Jason probably got Coke & candy. Shawn & Amanda knew more about food, they are vegetarian. They chose better than us. I can't remember what Alex did. Nathan went to a grocery store, bought individual-wrapped cheese & a pack of bologna. He made a sandwich in the van and put everything back in the un-iced cooler. On the onset this is not a bad plan.

There are moments when giving each other shit is simply a method to pass time. An amazing source of fun. It stems from skating. Maybe from being a punk. Yeah, it's mean. Whatever.

So let's go back a step. While Nathan is at the grocery store, Jason is Shoe Goo'ing a penny and a nickel to the dashboard of our van. He is not asking if it's OK to do this. It seems like a bit of a social experiment. Nathan's parents have generously bought this 1986 light-blue Chevrolet Sportvan in support of Nathan's music ventures. Nathan has generously supplied this punk house on wheels to all of us. Shoe Goo is killer. It's duct tape for Vans. Bologna going sour in the cooler, It wasn't long before broke Nathan was trying to rip the penny and the nickel off the dash for a next meal.

I can't remember where we slept that night.

—DAVE

"SO, ARE YOU GUYS STRAIGHT EDGE?"

As the second tour fizzed along, we got frustrated and began to focus on a common goal. Fortunately for us, the urgent need to rescue the summer with a little weed happened just as we rolled into Boulder, Colorado.

—ALEX

USA #2

tire plugs afforded
another chance to blow it
the second time around
down to 66 bucks
somewhere on 70
800 miles out
where commitment and math
have crashed
and neither adds up

discussion swerves to
calling it quits: skip the last
week-long dog-leg limp
past the lakes for one
straight shot home

15 hours and it's over

—JASON

THE BLACK BOW ON THE CASKET

The first tour made us a band. The second tour exposed our dysfunction. The few great shows we had couldn't outweigh the shitty ones, or the canceled ones that left us stranded and broke. Maybe as a result of this, personal and interpersonal issues flared. Nathan may have presented as the wobbliest wheel, but he was not the only one: I was being a hyper-aggressive dick, Shawn was mostly checked out. Alex was always a sweetie, but that wasn't glue enough to hold it all together. When Dave tagged along in California, it was a breath of fresh air in a stale van. Even as we plotted our demise, things got fun again . . . for a minute.

Amanda had already booked us studio time at Inner Ear, so recording the last batch of new songs upon our return would be the black bow on the casket before burying Swiz deep.

The idea was floated for Fury to piggyback the session; kick in the little bit of cash earned from their two shows and use whatever reel tape remained once Swiz finished basic tracks. Chris popped in and Fury charged through our 6 songs in one live, uninterrupted pass. It was the only time I noticed Eli get excited about what was going on through the glass. I put down a second guitar the same way. All told, tracking and mixing took maybe an hour. That was the last time Fury played together.

Shawn, Alex and I pretty much railroaded Nathan into agreeing to put a Fury track on the Swiz album. He said, "Fine . . . but at least let me fix Shawn's fuckups," and we were like, ". . . No."

Compared to the collective gusto when tracking the first Swiz album the year before, the vibe in the studio during *Hell Yes I Cheated* ran from crabby to grim. But I was surprised by—and proud of—the end result. Despite all the things that weren't working in our band, I didn't want to be done. I was happy to learn Alex and Shawn felt the same.

—JASON

HELL YES I CHEATED PHOTOS: 2

The flip-side photo for *Hell Yes* was shot in NYC during the fall of 1989. Nathan had recently moved there, having been dropped off over summer on the way home from our ill-fated second US tour. He had to come back down to D.C. that August as an expat to record the album, which was intended to be the last thing we did as a band (the photo shoot being a bit of loose-end busywork for the posthumous release).

Based on the art direction we had brainstormed, we needed to be in an old-school Italian restaurant—dressed to the nines—being served by a maître d' played by Billy D. of American Standard. So Shawn, Alex and I drove up to NYC where we met Nathan and his photographer friend Theresa. We all walked around St. Marks Place in our suits, looking for an Italian restaurant in the heart of "Curry Row."

There aren't any, so we settled on an empty Indian restaurant.

After the shoot we got high together in Nathan's apartment, which didn't really help the second logistical loose end for the night: to tell Nathan that, despite our formerly unanimous decision to break up, Shawn Alex, and I were going to continue Swiz with Dave.

Nathan was blindsided and bummed. We cited his disinterest in touring and the fact that he lived 4 hours away now. He felt strongly that if the band was going to continue, he wanted to be in it. I countered lamely with, ". . . But Dave already bought a bass."

I think at this point Nathan must've pieced together why, a month prior, we had suggested he sell the van to Dave. He went kinda dark and said, "Oh . . . I see how this is."

—JASON

Hell Yes I Cheated photo shoot #2
Fall 1989
Photos: Theresa Kelliher

KODAK TMZ 5054
KODAK TMZ 5054
KODAK TMZ 5054
KODAK TMZ 5054
7
9A
10
DAK TMZ 5054
10A
11
KODAK TMZ 5054
11A
8
KODAK TMZ 5054
35A
36
KODAK TMZ 5054
36A
15A
16
KODAK TMZ 5054
16A
17
17A
KODAK TMZ 5054
14
14A
15
15A

CARVIN

Chapter

EIGHT *(With Dave)*

YOUR EYES ARE DRIFTING

as he lies in violence
and I'm so confused
cuz it's my first time.
This was his moment
you were so damn ready
well now it's over.

—DAVE

Dave, the Rathskeller, Boston, MA
January 28,1990
Photo: Nicole Jean DiGiorgi-Chavez

BBQ IGUANA

Nathan decided to go to NY after that second tour. I went back to LA. Jason and I are on the phone talking about the end of Swiz. As many of our talks go, we're veering off in less dramatic directions particularly on the subject of cool guitars, Firebirds, then Thunderbirds, it's decided if I get a Thunderbird & move back to D.C., Swiz will continue.

Seemed like the longest bass I ever touched. Didn't actually sound that good. I don't think we cared. It was a solid excuse to rescue our favorite music. *My* favorite music.

I moved back to D.C.–Thunderbird, a bag of clothes, few other randoms. Jason (I think) got me into a group house on 13th Street. Mark Sullivan lived there. I didn't know him, but I worshipped King Face and was intimidated by the idea I could run into him in the hall. He's an elder of my DCHC memory.

I put one item on my wall, actually leaning on the fireplace mantel in my room. Mark wandered in one day, picked it up, surprised. I'd been listening to that record every day for months. He was magnetically pulled to it and questioned me on it. It was a copy of *Let There Be Rock*. Seems like most in D.C. had margin rock moments. Jason had KISS, I bought Nugent records cause I'd heard Ian and Jeff were into them. Although King Face tore through "Ain't Talkin' 'Bout Love" every show, I never put 'em in a rock category, it was just music I wanted. Mark & I bonded over *Let There Be Rock*. It made me love AC/DC more. Later, when I decided to move back to LA for school, Mark made me a mixtape, titled, "Go west young man." I couldn't have received anything cooler from him.

I bought Andy Rapoport's SVT Time Bomb amp. We started practicing. We got a show at the BBQ Iguana. There was now a deadline for having my shit together. Jason and I sat in front of each other, unplugged/plugged in the basement/bedroom, teaching me Nathan. I changed some. Learning Nathan is hard. His bass seemed on another level from what I have. Much to Jason's dismay, I never understood that Bootsy moment in "Ghost." Sorry, Nathan. I love the way it sounds but I can't play it.

I was in another band a year earlier, 8Ball with Kevin Haley and Steve Ramos. We needed a bass player. Jason and Shawn came to one of our practices. I asked if I could borrow Nathan to help 8Ball get going. They agreed and we started practicing in Jason's basement with Steve on Alex's kit. Nathan immediately knew what to do with our "Too Fast For Love" punk. Our first gig opening for King Face. Then Nathan couldn't do it anymore. So we returned him to the Swiz library, Adam Rapoport (Andy from King Face's brother) replaced him. 8Ball lasted 3 shows (Kevin, Adam & I all played in the Tigers together . . . history)

The night before the BBQ show, I was sitting in the Swiz van outside 4510 playing the songs to a tape, and Shawn came over and said something that made me feel a part of the band. I can't remember what but I was excited I'd made the whole move back from LA. Aside from hanging out with American Standard, the BBQ show wasn't actually memorable. At least not as much as some others. The stage was awkwardly high. I didn't recognize anyone there, which wasn't that out of the norm for Swiz playing D.C.

—DAVE

8ball, 9:30 Club, Washington, D.C.
Circa 1988
Photographer : Unknown

"YES, I WANT TO MOVE UP THE TCBY LADDER!"

I was really happy for Nathan when he moved to New York. Unlike me, someone who bailed on going to school up there to play in a band, Nathan seemed naturally drawn to New York. He was an artist. He was a wiseass. He had a relentless intellect.

Why wouldn't he live there?

We still kept in touch for a while and his stories about getting hired at TCBY and being mesmerized by the hiring manager's pitch ("Yes, I want to move up the TCBY ladder!") got me laughing so hard I almost hyperventilated.

Nathan started playing with Shudder to Think, a group I loved, and one that had shared stages with Swiz a whole lot on our second tour. Craig, their singer, and Nathan were really tight and had worked at an ice cream store's pushcart in Georgetown as teenagers. Shudder went on a different trajectory. They did big tours, got a record deal. That's a story I know little about. But the experience was pretty far removed from what I was doing, and Nathan and I drifted apart.

I don't think anyone could have stepped in on bass when Nathan left. Anyone except Dave. He was a friend of Jason's for years. He had traveled with the band, and his affable presence smoothed over a lot of rough edges. I spent many nights with Jason waiting for Dave to get off from his busboy stint at Malarkey's, a Bethesda bar, so we could engage in some mischief or another. Dave was already part of the group. He just needed to get the bass lines down.

—ALEX

NATHAN . . . SORRY, BABY

There was tension with Nathan. I don't remember exactly, but I felt . . . I don't know, should we break up? You need decide what you're going to hold on to, what you're going to let go of . . . how much you're going to invest in that fucking shit, you know what I mean?

I don't remember feeling like I was betraying Nathan or anything like that because it felt like he was cheating on us, man. I thought there was some crossover with Shudder to Think into the Swiz time where he'd been fucking like, pretty much playing with those guys. I might be wrong. I probably am.

Either way, as talented as Nathan was and was proving himself to be, his enthusiasm for the band was not there anymore . . . Dave was hungry. So at that point, I was just like, "Nathan . . . sorry, baby. That's the music biz, son. Yeah, I know it's rough on the streets, man. Trust me, I know . . . I've been there . . . I'm still a little blurry from my own wound."

—SHAWN

FUN AGAIN . . . FOR A MINUTE

I was so psyched to get my best friend Dave in the band. He had already been there from the beginning: roadie, supporter, riff contributor, buddy with a penchant for grabbing a mic to sing along during our sets. It made perfect sense to have him pick up the bass rather than us pull the plug on it all. I had hopes that this shot in the arm would cure all that ailed us.

Sure enough, like his visit on the last tour, things got fun again . . .

. . . for a minute.

—*JASON*

SPIDEY

I don't really feel like I was threatened by Dave. When you're that age and you're fucking hanging out with people, sometimes you just focus on, like, the main personalities surrounding whatever you're doing, and everything else is on the side. Not saying I thought Dave was like some fucking dork or whatever, or, you know, like a punk or some shit like that. I was just like, *Oh yeah, Jason's sidekick "Spidey."*

But when he joined the band and, I mean, stepped the fuck *up* . . . well, with any shared experience you get to see more of a person, and I think that's what built our friendship. I was super stoked and thankful we had another solid bass player, but also, Dave came out as a full of person to me in the experience of being able to play in a band with him.

—*SHAWN*

D.C. SPACE

I played d.c. space with Swiz. Out of almost everywhere in D.C., I think I loved the space most. Maybe even more than Wilson Center. We saw so many shows there—Rapeman (Nathan got us in; I think he was the only one of us who knew Big Black at the time), Rollins spoken word (surprisingly hilarious), & every D.C. band you could think of. Embrace—I think it was their first show. Incredible to see Ian basically singing in the Faith at d.c. space. Anyone who's ever loved the Embrace record, I wish you could have seem them live. They played everything faster. Dear Ian, please let Brian Baker remix the Embrace record like he's been wandering around muttering about all these years. Ian's Embrace lyric sheet was handed out as we entered the door at d.c. space that night. I think he spit on us while singing and we were cool with that.

Typical night was: speeding to Fort Reno from Bethesda (pass out flyers while not paying attention to the weird band we'd never heard of and trying to talk to girls), then speeding to d.c. space (see a band we did like / hang out in front of d.c. space not looking cool, trying to talk to girls), then speed to Georgetown Café for wee-hours-night breakfast. During one of these episodes Shawn and I were wrestling in the van (no seat-belt law yet), and I punched his knee and broke my hand. That night we went to Sibley Hospital, not night breakfast.

Christ, did I play d.c. space with Swiz? Maybe it was a dream.

—DAVE

Show flyer
February 21, 1989
Art: Jason Farrell
Courtesy of Shannon McIntyre Bugos

NINE

When I joined Swiz I had "Nine." At least most of it. This wasn't my first contribution. I'd been in the basement messing around one day, then Swiz all came down to practice so I had to clear out. I'd been playing some riff; Jason asked me if he could have it and turned it into "Dave's Song" on *Hell Yes*. I was stoked even though I tried to play it cool and even though it seemed like an afterthought on the record.

Everything those guys did to "Nine" made it better. I didn't have a chorus, so Jason got me to spit something out and he proceeded to put that sick Damned kinda line over it. I think Alex came up with the ending.

Shawn's lyrics—period.

We played "Nine" for the first time in NY. ABC No Rio? I can't remember. I think the show got moved at the last minute. Nathan was there. It's easy to admit I was super nervous playing those songs in front of him (he also stood right in the front). After we played he positively commented on "Nine." That made that show for me.

—DAVE

Swiz, Lismar Lounge, New York, NY
February 24, 1990
Photo: Nicole Jean DiGiorgi-Chavez

Marshall
Los Angeles
Raiders

BIG BAD WOLF: PART 1

Another midday matinee. A bar somewhere in Pennsylvania . . . maybe Delaware. Upon arrival we learned that a warm-up gig for an up-and-coming hair-metal band called Big Bad Wolf had been shoehorned by the club into the middle of our hardcore bill. Despite the obvious genre disconnect, the band members were nice and chatty as we all set up and got sounds. A few confused show attendees filtered into the space, and the forgettable event was underway.

Big Bad Wolf was pretty good at what they do. They took it in stride when Dave jumped onstage with his unplugged Thunderbird and fully rocked out Angus-style to their cover of "Walk All Over You." Dave did this with 100% conviction and commitment, so it was hard for anyone to tell if he was making fun of them or truly moved by the moment (I knew it was the latter). After they ran the rest of their set choreography, they packed and left for their evening show, which left the club itself five people closer to empty.

Naturally, we made fun of them during our set . . . how could we not?

This irritated the soundman, a hair afficionado himself. Later, as we waited to get paid, he leaned from his raised booth and laid into Alex for us having showed a lack of respect toward a real band. The volume and intensity of their exchange escalated until the soundman was strained out over his railing yelling straight down into Alex's confused face, berating Swiz as being unprofessional shit . . . not half the band that Big Bad Wolf was.

Shawn, who had been passively watching up till this point, stood up and spat in the soundman's face.

—JASON

BIG BAD WOLF: PART 2

The soundman exploded. The volume of his screams dipped only momentarily, as if on a fader, when he disappeared down his back ladder. He came back louder a second later as he rounded the corner and charged. Before he could cover the short distance between him and Shawn, it quickly filled with bar staff.

The soundman tried to fight through the arms that held him back, the spit still glistening on his face. A fat bouncer materialized, scooped Shawn up like a mannequin, and walked him briskly out the side exit, pulling with him the whole amoeba of commotion that burst into the parking lot under an afternoon sun.

Shawn was thrown, but stuck his landing in an exaggerated fighting stance reminiscent of a boxer from the previous century: low and wide, with fists curled back toward himself . . . like an Irish cartoon mascot replete with flared eyes and jutted chin. The appearance was ridiculous, terrifying, and entirely effective; his nonverbal challenge was not taken up. The soundman, bouncer, and Shawn stood frozen in this triangular stalemate as Alex, Dave, and I gingerly wove our way through them toward the van.

—JASON

CRUSHED / A BEAUTIFUL BLUR

I loved our gig at Club Pizazz 2 in Philly with Absolution. Even though the stage was slippery. Gavin was cool to me.

I loved the weekend we did in Rhode Island and Boston with Killing Time, formerly Raw Deal. They wore rugby shirts. NYHC confused me. I think the Boston show was at the Rat. A highlight. I feel like we just crushed. Kids were cascading over the foot-high stage. It felt good to be in this gang.

I loved our show in Rhode Island with Verbal Assault at the Living Room. I'd never been so nervous. I told Jason I didn't think I could play. We had to walk through the crowd with our instruments to get to the stage. It was packed. I remember my first foot landing on the stage—all the nervous left and the show was a beautiful blur. VA went on and destroyed. Pete Chramiec's guitar sound was incredible. I loved *ON*.

There was some gig in Virginia. Shawn didn't see it, but a handful of nazis fucked with him while we played. Dumb. After some show Shawn and the guy running the club almost came to blows. Sucked. Shawn can drop into a fight stance lightning fast, it's actually scary. Makes you glad he's on your side. Rad.

—DAVE

WEEKEND BOYS' CLUB

Hardcore in the early '90s didn't feel like hardcore or punk rock to me anymore, it was too tough-guy oriented. It felt like a weekend boys' club, you had to wear tough-guy armor all the time. In D.C. there were remnants of skinhead gangs that morphed into hip-hop thug-core type crews and I didn't feel like I identified with any straight edge crews either, so I was really tired of it . . . When the gang element entered I really couldn't fuck with it anymore.

—SHAWN✷✦

SLIDE

Walter called me in the spring of 1990 to ask if Swiz wanted to tour Europe as a package with his new band, Quicksand. He had fresh connections, having just pulled it off with Gorilla Biscuits or maybe Youth of Today, but at that point his new band hadn't released anything yet, so maybe they couldn't swing it alone.

I was so excited I went out and immediately applied for a passport. Dave and Alex were also psyched. When I spoke to Shawn, he seemed reluctant for some reason. I hadn't considered that this was something I'd have to talk him into, but I tried to make the case and left him to think on it. He came back sometime later saying he would not be going—something about not letting his boss down at the bike shop—but he'd be fine with us getting someone else to sing if we wanted to go so bad. That's when I knew we were not aligned anymore and it was just a matter of time till it all dissolved.

We had the Anthrax scheduled and nothing after it, so at practice Dave, Alex, and I decided to make that the last show. The NY/CT scene was always good for us, more so than D.C. Ending it there seemed to make enough sense. Shawn wasn't privy to the decision . . . he was kinda checked out at that point and rarely made it to practices anyway. For some reason we didn't mention it during the 5-hour drive to Connecticut, either. Only when we got to the venue and Shawn saw the flyers saying *I'll Never Love Again* did he realize that this would be our last show.

My passport eventually came in the mail. I didn't get to use it for another seven years.

—JASON

Jason's passport
Issued April 1990
Courtesy of the Department of State

PARALYSIS

When Swiz broke up I was bummed. Those guys got 3 years out of it. I got a bump over 1. Nathan got 2. Amanda got everything but the Jade Tree segment.

I hadn't had enough. I wasn't ready to be done.
I was annoyed with, "Is is now was, gonna do is done."

Shawn was falling for cycling. Alex wrote the lyrics to "Paralysis," which explained our end. Jason wanted one more show. He needed a definitive ending.

So we got this show up in Connecticut at the Anthrax with American Standard and HR's reggae band. It felt weird to me. Jason made a cool flyer. Still felt weird. The show itself, I don't really remember it. I think this was the show Matt Dolan ran into Bill Dolan and cut his head. Darryl Jenifer borrowed my SVT and played it louder than I thought was possible. After HR, I think Super Touch played.

HR was walking around the Anthrax. He was followed by a beautiful woman in a striking red dress holding a bag of weed. They were walking all over. HR smoking. Lady in red holding the bag. It was a sight.

I had no idea where the other Swiz guys were. Jason and I started following HR and the lady. Finally in some room filled with punks, HR turned around, looked at us, and said, "Now, how did I know you wanted some of this?" We couldn't speak. (He's the singer of the freakin' Bad Brains and now a beautiful lady in red follows him around with drugs—we were overwhelmed.) Jason made an affirmative head motion. HR got us high. I'll never forget Jason's red eyes. Mine looked the same.

This was my Swiz end.

—DAVE

RENT/JOBS/RESPONSIBILITIES: PART 2 (1990)

It was a relief when the band ended.
I was really tired.
I felt like I needed to
find a job and make money
so I could just get an apartment.
We weren't really sure where it was going
or where it *could* go from there.

—*SHAWN*

Swiz with Bill, Rathskeller, Boston, MA
January 28,1990
Photo: Nicole Jean DiGiorgi-Chavez

SHAWN

I'LL NEVER LOVE

Chapter 9

CODA

DESCRIBE THE GHOST

The time has come
to sit in chairs and
talk about motion

conjure its form
from dust blown off
old receipts

prod it to parade around
the attic rafters so we can
describe the ghost:

an anachronism
not vengeful, not sad, just
befuddled by the interim

—JASON

Show flyer, last show, detail of original art
August 3, 1990
Art: Jason Farrell

ALL MY LIES ARE TRUE: PART 3

My time with Swiz brought a lot of First Times, Never Agains, and Lasting Impressions. Starting with the obvious: the chance to travel to out-of-town shows, meeting people from all over, and seeing the US and Canada. The not so obvious or even really believable was that I got my driver's license in order to do so. I had had no interest in getting my license, and in fact had renewed my learner's permit, and it was set to expire before the '88 tour opportunity came about. So my real learning was on the highways from show to show.

Here are some others:

- Finding myself with them, mixed up in a brawl, at a show where we were being advanced upon by people we had been hanging out with
- Cliff jumping
- Hanging out in a recording studio
- Being propositioned by promoters
- Speeding tickets
- West Texas
- Getting harassed by cops (true story: in Mississippi, the officer came in and shut down the show because he couldn't hear the Little League game across the street.)
- Ace Frehley
- Screening shirts
- Reading rooms and sizing people up
- The kindness of most and the shittiness of some

- Sunrise in Montana
- Stars late at night in the deserts of Arizona
- A band enters the stage by way of a hearse driven into the venue
- Feeling what it is like to have a tire blow out on the highway
- The enthusiasm of production
- The infection of collaboration
- Mötley Crüe, Metallica, Megadeth, Skid Row, Poison . . .
- Skate parks in warehouses in the middle of the country
- Broad & Ripple and Midwestern hanging out
- Pirate radio
- Casinos
- A double-wide show venue
- Show venue in a cornfield
- Show in a squat stealing electricity
- All the actual kids and "kids" who made shows happen in their cities and towns; finding or creating spaces for bands to play, then feeding and housing them; and the parents who opened their homes for the bands to have a place to stay

(To be continued . . .)

—AMANDA

EXTRACTION

Getting into Swiz was the easy part.
Extracting myself was a bit more difficult.

I don't remember how the Swiz intro happened, but I knew Ramsey and he put it all together. What followed was countless practices at Jason's house, about 100 shows, new friends both in the band and not, going through a heady first love, going through the tension of independence from/dependence on my parents, seeing a million new sights in a big big land, feeling saved that certain band members were alongside me, frustrated at times that others were too, realizing everyone probably felt the same way, and coming out of the whole experience wanting more, feeling lost that it wasn't happening, and settling into a long frustration, convinced that I had made music the one way it was supposed to be done and I could never surpass the pride and ownership of something I was a part of with Swiz.

My own definition was wrapped up in the band, and why not? For all of the antagonisms and uncertainty of playing as a group, what we did was close to a perfect reflection of what I envisioned as a band at the time. And some people responded.

That was a bit of a trip for a teenager. I was at my sister's college graduation weekend in Providence in 1989, and my brother and I struck up a conversation with a skater guy in the 7-Eleven parking lot. I told him my band was coming up the following week for a show.

"What band?" he asked, seeming a bit blasé and half-interested.

With my one-syllable reply—"Swiz"—his eyes opened wide, and he dropped to the asphalt of the lot as if I had just knocked the breath out of him. I felt the same way! I loved the band.

What I found when the band dissolved was that it was hard to move on. Hard to move to new relationships, hard to play new music, hard to find fun in sitting behind the drums. Hard to be happy. I didn't want to play the same music we played in Swiz, but I wanted to identify as tightly and completely with the people and music as I did with Swiz.

The Swiz guys have seen me at my worst. They have seen my faults, they've seen me freak out, have an angry fit, be insecure. I've seen them act ridiculously too! My late teens and early 20s were made easier by this group of people. I've had the pleasure of seeing them at different intervals over the years. I love how they've grown. I think I have too. They are a constant touchstone.

It's a long story, but somehow I came to both appreciate how creative and talented the people I was surrounded by were in those years, just as I met and experienced new relationships that were also rewarding. And I learned that another way to enjoy music was to let go, not clench so tightly, and have fun.

—ALEX †

WISDOM AND BULLSHIT

Having a shared experience like Swiz is gift enough, and then having the further gift of seeing this experience documented/discussed/parsed over, with empathy, from multiple perspectives . . . I want to acknowledge that this is such a rare privilege. I'm struck by the intelligence and the strength of character of my old friends here.

To you, my friends, to all the elders at whose feet I sat, absorbing wisdom and bullshit: I say thank you.

We can't be told. We must break a bone, and then do it again, and again. We can only hope those broken bones heal properly, and that's the gamble.

Somebody once said advice is a form of nostalgia, a way of fishing old experiences out of the trash and selling them for more than they're worth. Earlier in this text, a version of me from perhaps twenty years back suggested I would tell my teenage self to hush.

Sitting here today with my tween son slouched over his phone (a skateboarder, in essence wearing evolved versions of the same clothes my friends and I wore back in the '80s), I'd want to modify the way I addressed my past self.

I'd tell me: Everything is going to be alright. Have a blast. None of this should be taken seriously. Be kind and do your best.

And I'd give myself a hug.

—*NATHAN*

UNCONSCIOUS

So we were creating—for lack of a better word—"art," but not being conscious of creating art . . . not realizing what it was and not classifying it like that when it was happening.

And now, looking back on it and thinking about it? Yeah, I don't know . . . I see its place in the fabric of American music, especially American music that was created in the 1980s—the derivatives of punk, hardcore, whatever you want to call it. Conscious or unconscious, that music has become an influence on a lot of people. I mean, not exclusive to us, but I think bands can kind of touch people in a certain way at a certain period of time that is just indelible. It's still there with everybody who experienced it, you know what I mean?

And when people discover it now, it's a good representation of the creativity that was going on back at that period of time. Maybe for younger people who are adjacent to members of that generation, it gives them a perspective into what those people were actually like when *they* were young, before they became an old fuddy-duddy or weirdo artist or whatever.

I definitely feel very proud of Swiz and what we made. Just even playing and all the small experiences, good and bad, inside of that . . . goddamn, I'd defend that band and stand for it with my life, man. Maybe I feel magical about it. Not sure how else to put it, because, I mean, it was like magic . . . what a crazy combination to come together and create what we crave. So all that makes me feel good. But it also makes me feel like kind of a weight or responsibility to that. It's a pretty powerful feeling. Like a blessing, and sometimes it feels like a little bit of a curse.

If I'm true to myself, I think, *Well, yeah, that's a piece of art that you created back then,* and you can get behind it and everything, maybe get a smile or two looking back at our youth and just thinking about like, *Wow, I did that.* But don't hold on to it too tight . . . you also have to have the ability to let it go.

—*SHAWN*

STRUCK BY THE RANDOMNESS

I'd see Tim Owen around Bethesda from time to time. He was in that youth crew of 1989 Safari Club kids, roughly the same age away from us as we were from the younger end of the Dischord spectrum. Years later he told me that Swiz was the first hardcore band he ever saw (opening for Youth of Today and Dag Nasty at the 9:30 Club in 1987), but I'd also known him even earlier than that as one of the more opinionated grommets who would frequent the skate shop where I worked.

After Swiz broke up, we were each focused elsewhere (Alex in Severin, Dave back in LA, Shawn at work), so our last recording languished on its reel at Inner Ear with no plans for release. Personally, I was burnt on bands and the scene in general. Aside from having dived into my first serious relationship, I was otherwise socially adrift, just working and trying to patch together a degree from the scattered college credits I'd been neglecting.

During that time, Tim would give me sporadic scene updates, tell me about new bands he thought showed continuity with our trajectory (Drive Like Jehu, John Henry West). He called me one day to let me know some Safari kids were trying to steal the name Fury . . . even gave me the singer's phone number to set it straight. They eventually changed their name to Battery (coincidentally, a name Swiz had considered and rejected years before).

The dude could network. It was like his superpower. I imagine that was useful when he and his friend Darren Walters launched their new label, Jade Tree. It was Tim who let me know Swiz had interest percolating in some circles, growing since our demise two years prior. He floated the idea of releasing the last Swiz recording as a 7" and a complete discography CD, putting all our songs under one pretty bow; a trend made possible by a drop in manufacturing costs and made kosher by Minor Threat. With our back catalog nearly out of print, we jumped at the idea.

Tim and Darren were trying to do things properly but may have been working with a lawyer unfamiliar with punk. They sent us a Xerox of a fax of a long-ass contract covering off *on in-perpetuity recoupments amortized at 6% against annuity* . . . maybe some shit about *mechanical sync license abatement in tertiary markets* . . . it may or may not have had *Jade Tree* penciled in above where *Geffen, Inc.* had been scratched out. Amanda took one look and urged us to erase our hasty signatures. We countered their offer with a piece of paper that basically said, *50/50 after expenses*, and, with the lawyer out of the way, we all moved happily forward.

Pairing up with Swiz gave Jade Tree just enough of a legitimacy boost to secure a spot with Mordam distribution. In return, Jade Tree saved Swiz from sliding off into oblivion. We are hugely in debt to Amanda and Sammich Records for steering Swiz while it was alive, and to Tim, Darren, and Jade Tree for resurrecting its ghost.

In revisiting this history, I'm struck by the randomness of it all—having been born and set in the same general area/era, a Venn diagram of semi-similar interests overlapping at one blind practice, halfway through which I knew I'd found something I wanted to invest myself in. By the end of that practice the other new teenage bandmates were echoing the same sentiment. It was that quick: one afternoon, one meeting . . . then all-in for a solid three-year run.

And I liked these guys: funny, fun, goofy, dead serious, thoughtful. Despite disagreements, fights, bouts of pettiness, and what felt like an insurmountable lack of interest from the music community, we still managed to be of one mission, one mind. And, for a few years, we would not be deterred.

Not saying this was unique to Swiz—like we tapped some secret, or that we felt this connection any stronger than any other band might. It was just the first time *I* felt it, and thus understood it could exist . . . that it *should* exist. As a result, we are all still friends 35+ years on, we all still play music . . . and some of us still play music together.

It's a little odd to me that some people still care about this band—its genesis, lifespan, and eventual taxidermy—there are far better bands and far better musicians. Can't always quantify why something floats your boat, but in bands that do it for me, I can hear a bit of that same sense of mission and connection within their songs.

—JASON †✦

PART 2: THE LAPSE

I turned this essay in last night to Jason, our natural leader—my first Swiz homework in many years. I blew some details. Here's my list of corrections:

- John Garrish and I rode up to the ramp in fall of 9th grade, not summer, more like October. Jason reminds me, Richard Basch is the one who brought punk to us. He arrived with tapes and spray-painted an "encyclopedic list of bands" on the ramp . . . mostly California bands. I remember the half-pipe looked like a large plywood high school Trapper Keeper. Funny, we owe a lot to Richard for focusing us at that incredibly impressionable age. I guess I commonly leave him out of my historic memory because he wasn't with us in 8th grade and he moved back to California before 10th. Jason tried to find him intermittently over the years. Richard, wherever are you, thank you for giving us Black Flag and the Circle Jerks (and many others, but those are the ones that froze me).

- Jason also remembers John and me showing up at the quarter-pipe behind the Japanese Steak House in Bethesda in the summer after 8th grade. Technically this would have been the first time we saw some type of vert-ish skate structure. It was in the parking lot by this crazy asphalt berm (like an earthquake just struck that one spot) that the local BMX kids un-politically-correctly abbreviated as the "Jap jump." (My kids are gonna disown me for writing that—Alice & Hazel, don't leave me, I need you.) I remember this episode happening after discovering Marcus's house, but I defer to Jason—he remembers Didgits lyrics. (Note: I would NOT recommend the '80s as a great teacher of how we should talk to or treat others. Please refer to a different decade for better behavior.)

- We played Club Pizazz 2 with Burn, not Absolution. Jason's definitely correct about this. Absolution's stuck in my mind because Alan Peters, bass player for Absolution, had the craziest rig ever. He'd lay an SVT cabinet on its side, put another one on top of it horizontally, then two 94lb. SVT heads on top of all that. The word *Absolution* was sprayed on his square wall of SVT. We talked about the rig after the Pizazz show. How did those dudes carry that stuff around?

- Dang it, this last one is the bummer memory that I obviously & completely rearranged in my brains. Apparently our last show was with Supertouch & American Standard, not HR's reggae band and American Standard. (Yeah, I spaced what bands Jason actually put on the "cool flyer"; I do remember he drew a ribbon on it that said, *I'll Never Love Again.*) This means the HR Anthrax show with the beautiful red-dress weed lady happened at the other & previous time we played the Anthrax. I didn't even remember we played there twice. My brains combined both shows. And apparently it combined two bands, too, because Darryl was *not* the bassist in HR, and could not have been the dude who borrowed my rig.

- Which also means my Swiz End memory with Jason riding off down 95, sunset bloodshot eyes, is not correct. The memories of what happened at the HR gig are correct, the timeline is off. I prefer the Bad Brains song "Supertouch" to the Supertouch band (sorry).

So fuckit, I'm gonna replace my final Swiz End with the Black Cat show.

In 2014, Scott Crawford asked us to play one of the shows for his D.C. punk documentary film, *Salad Days*. In discussion we were conflicted. After the Anthrax we had a pact to never play again under the name *Swiz*. (Sweetbelly Freakdown is proof. Terrible name, fun record to make, thank you J. Robbins, I loved making noise in your basement.) After many cross-country discussions we agreed to play as long as our name could be kept off the bill and held a secret. (Honestly, what the f is wrong with us? . . . Sometimes we're the dumbest nonsensical punks on the planet.) Scott musta wanted to kill us . . . Dear Scott, if you are reading, you were very nice to put up with our shit; on behalf of Swiz, I thank you. (We've known Scott since he was 10 or 12 and we were 15 or 17.)

The show was killer. It was packed. My friend Chris came from Philly. Soulside pulls folks outta the woodwork. Shawn's first words—"None of these bands would be here without Amanda MacKaye. This show is for you, Amanda."

This is why I love all in this band so much. There's a certain indescribable sensitivity in all of us to include crucial details at clutch moments. To remember where we come from. To spread the pride & aesthetic of punk as much as the music we love and were raised on. That Shawn moment propelled me through the set. (Right before we climbed the stage, Brian Baker & Andy Rapoport, looking down at me with that go-do-your-rock-duty-or-go-home look, said, "Try to look cool"—that helped a bit also.)

I'd secretly reached out to Nathan to see if he wanted to play some of the set. It woulda been cool to have us all in the same spot for this amazing reunion/post-existence homecoming. It also seemed like a super fun idea. He was in London and couldn't participate. I selfishly kept all the bass fun for myself.

It was amazing to play in front of a sold-out Black Cat. Alex was awkwardly high on the Black Cat drum riser. I loved seeing him play those songs again. We share the same birthday. Although I don't believe Alex and I ever achieved the perfect cross between the Captain/Rat, Chuck/Robo, or Baker/Nelson. Alex's wit sliced through the sometimes pretentious/overly serious side of hardcore at usually just the right time. He looked nervous that night and that was comforting to me as I was feeling the same. I saw Dante there and talked to him for the first time in many years. The sight of him makes me feel like it's 1987 at a d.c. space Ignition show.

We played Void, "Think." We played Fury, "Resurrection." We played one of my favorite songs—Government Issue, "Familiar." I secretly hoped John Stabb was there to witness. I saw G.I. a hundred times, I never met him. *Joy Ride* is in my top 3. This show went down like I'd wanted our gigs to go 30 years ago.

I loved it.

—*DAVE*

t.c.t.p.

A sincere thank you to the photographers who contributed their images, the people who shared their flyers, and the interviewers who shared their transcripts for this project.

An equally sincere apology to any photographers whose names may have become mismatched or detached from their photos in the decades since having taken them.

Thank you to our friends who came to see us, to the bands we shared stages with, and to our families who allowed space for us to practice (the Farrells, Danielses, Larsons, and Metcalfs).

Thank you to the people and labels past and present who put out or helped fund our records: Amanda, Eli, and Sammich; Tim, Darren, and Jade Tree; Jason Parker and THD; Ian, Jeff, and Dischord.

We would like to personally thank Michelle; Chloe and Ian; Chris and Gabriel; Nina and Nils; Allen and Arlo; Celeste, Alice, and Hazel; Paul, Spencer, and Pekkanen; Bill, Matt, J, and Supe.

A huge thank you to Johnny and Akashic Books for putting this out.

Right:
Jason and Shawn, South Carolina
July 6, 1989
Photo: Alex Daniels

Back cover:
Swiz, the Rathskeller, Boston, MA
January 28, 1990
Photo: Nicole Jean DiGiorgi-Chavez